50 Ways
to Understand
Communication

50 Ways to Understand Communication

A Guided Tour of Key Ideas and Theorists in
Communication, Media, and Culture

Arthur Asa Berger

With Illustrations by the Author

ROWMAN & LITTLEFIELD PUBLISHERS, INC.
Lanham • Boulder • New York • Toronto • Oxford

ROWMAN & LITTLEFIELD PUBLISHERS, INC.

Published in the United States of America
by Rowman & Littlefield Publishers, Inc.
A wholly owned subsidiary of The Rowman & Littlefield Publishing Group, Inc.
4501 Forbes Boulevard, Suite 200, Lanham, Maryland 20706
www.rowmanlittlefield.com

P.O. Box 317, Oxford OX2 9RU, UK

British Library Cataloguing in Publication Information Available

Library of Congress Cataloging-in-Publication Data

Berger, Arthur Asa, 1933–
     50 ways to understand communication : a guided tour of key ideas and theorists in communication, media, and culture / Arthur Asa Berger.
           p.   cm.
     Includes bibliographical references and index.
     ISBN-13: 978-0-7425-4107-8 (cloth : alk. paper)
     ISBN-10: 0-7425-4107-X (cloth : alk. paper)
     ISBN-13: 978-0-7425-4108-5 (paper : alk. paper)
     ISBN-10: 0-7425-4108-8 (paper : alk. paper)
     1. Communication.   I. Title: Fifty ways to understand communication.
     II. Title.

P90.B4128   2006
302.23—dc22

                                        2005031253

Printed in the United States of America

The paper used in this publication meets the minimum requirements of American National Standard for Information Sciences—Permanence of Paper for Printed Library Materials, ANSI/NISO Z39.48-1992.

Contents

Acknowledgments

I want to thank my editor, Brenda Hadenfeldt, for her help with this book and her continued support. I greatly appreciate her efforts on my behalf. I also wish to express my appreciation to the four professors who reviewed the manuscript, whose names I don't know, for their ideas—many of which I've incorporated into this book. In addition, I owe a great debt of gratitude to Professor Francisco Yus of Alicante University in Spain, who was kind enough to comment on a number of the selections in the book. I have inserted several of his comments into the text as personal communication. Finally, let me express my thanks to my copy editor, Patricia Zylius, my production editor, April Leo, and all the other people at Rowman & Littlefield who helped with the production of this book. It takes the assistance of a considerable number of people to publish a book, and I'm grateful for everyone's help with bringing *50 Ways to Understand Communication: A Guided Tour of Key Ideas and Theorists in Communication, Media, Culture* into existence. I have included a bibliography and glossary adapted from my book *Media & Society* to provide readers with additional sources of information.

Introduction: How You Can Use This Book

his book is designed for undergraduate students taking courses in communication, media, and cultural studies. It was written to be used as a text for professors who want to provide their students with an overview of some of the key theories, statements, and arguments in these interrelated fields. And there is a logic to the way it is organized.

I recall reading about a French avant-garde novelist who wrote a novel in which each chapter appeared on a different card. Readers could shuffle the cards and come up with a "new" novel each time, though of course what was new was only the arrangement of the chapters. But the arrangement of elements in a narrative makes a big difference in the way readers interpret dialogue and events that take place in it.

To Dream an Impossible Dream

The task I have undertaken is to offer fifty short statements by writers and scholars of all kinds, about different aspects of communication, including the mass media of communication, that are—in my opinion—central to understanding what communication is, how it works, and what effects it might have on individuals and on culture and society. This book is, in one sense, a Quixotic venture, or perhaps even an impossible task, because scholars and experts in all fields of communication and media studies will ask, with good reason, why a certain article or book is not represented in my list. The reason I offer is that I chose the selections because I thought they provided the best and most interesting overall picture of communication, media, and culture, and are the most useful ideas, concepts, and theories for my readers to consider.

I have taken the liberty, in some cases, of selecting passages from an author that are a page or two separated from one another in the original publication, but I indicate this with ellipses. I have also edited out names of authors and books in some cases and made other minor editorial adjustments to facilitate readability, but I have never changed the meaning of a passage. I have, on some occasions, rearranged the order in which material is found in the works from which I quote—to make the selection more cogent. I have also provided a bibliography that lists a number of books for students to investigate if they wish to pursue their interests in communication, media, and cultural studies.

The Complexities of Watching Television, Going to the Movies, and More

When we watch television or go to the movies, we actually process a great deal of information with incredible speed. We listen to the dialogue and the way it is spoken. We look at the facial expressions of the characters, notice what they are wearing, pay attention to their body language, consider the surroundings in which the action in a story is taking place, think about the symbolic significance of the characters and the places where various events happen, listen to the music in the background, pay attention to sound effects, and do a hundred other things—with great speed and generally without being fully aware of what we are doing.

It All Starts with the Word

These are the subjects I have dealt with in this book. It all starts with words. After all, what we call dialogue (or lyrics in songs) involves words spoken between characters. In everyday life, we call this conversation. And it turns out that conversation is a much more complicated matter than we might imagine.

So I've dealt with media in a somewhat different way than many books on the subject by focusing on communication concepts that we can use to better understand the texts (the academic term for films, television shows, advertisements, songs, and so on) we watch when we watch a television show, see a movie, watch a music video, or play a video game.

In *50 Ways to Understand Communication: A Guided Tour of Key Ideas and Theorists in Communication, Media, and Culture*, I offer fifty short selections, generally under 300 words, from scholars who provide us with key concepts and insights that will be useful to us in analyzing and interpreting texts and the role of the media in society. I have taken considerable care to arrange the selections in what, in my mind, is a coherent order. Professors using this book can, of course, alter the way the chapters are read. But there is, I suggest, a logic to my arrangement of selections. I start with what, for all practical purposes, can be considered the most basic element in verbal communication—the word. I have several selections dealing with words per se and others dealing with what happens when we string words together and make sentences that we use in conversing with others.

The core element in visual communication is the sign, and I offer a selection on signs (and several others that, to varying degrees, deal with signs) and the science that explains how they work—semiotics. The Greek term *semeion* means "sign."

I include some selections that deal with language in general and with certain aspects of language, such as metaphor, gender differences in the way language is used, and black speech. In addition, I offer a discussion of nonverbal language. Facial expression and body language convey a great deal of information to us. This information is of use to us in conversing with others but also in trying to understand attitudes and motivations of characters in mass-mediated texts such as films, television shows, commercials, and videos.

This material is followed by discussions of symbolism, an important part of our daily lives and of texts of all kinds. Symbols speak to the unconscious elements in our psyches and have great power over us, so it is important to understand something about symbolism. These discussions involve phenomena such as everyday objects, mythic characters (Miss America, for example), and fashion.

A large number of the selections are devoted to the media in a direct manner. Thus I have material on topics such as hot and cool media, the way media affect our minds, the way the media portray people of color, the importance of narratives in the media, the power of rock music, the role of digital media, the impact of cell telephones in creating "smart mobs," and postmodernism and the media.

The last set of selections deals with the role of the arts, including mass-mediated works of art (what I've called texts), in society. There are many different theories about the role of art of all kinds in society, and so I conclude the book with material on this subject. These discussions will help us deal with considerations about how mass-mediated culture or pop culture differs from so-called elite culture, and the role and function of the arts and the media in society.

All of these selections deal either directly or indirectly (and implicitly) with texts and the media that carry them and will be of use to students who want to understand why it is that a movie or a song or a television show has the impact on them that it has. I've always felt that works of art, in all media and of all kinds, are actually incredibly complex and work in many different ways. Reading this book will help you understand better how texts work and the role that the medium that carries them (or the media in general) plays in our lives and our societies.

It should give you a good overview of communication, media, and culture (all of which are related to one another) and put you in contact with some of the best and most fertile minds working in these areas. I hope that after reading some of these selections you might want to read the books from which they come and explore the ideas you read about in more depth. Whatever the case, I believe you'll find there's a great deal to think about in the material I have selected for you. I believe that the concepts and ideas I've dealt with in this book will be of interest and of use to you and help you understand better the various complexities involved in communication and the related fields of media and cultural studies—in all their forms and manifestations.

James Beniger (1990), a communications scholar at the Annenberg School for Communication at the University of Southern California, wrote an article titled "Who Are the Most Important Theorists of Communication?" It lists the number of citations of communication theorists that appeared in The International Encyclopedia of Communication, an 1800-page work published by the Oxford University Press. The top twelve theorists are listed below, in order of the number of times they were mentioned in the encyclopedia. I have placed the names of theorists whose ideas are cited in this book in boldface.

1. **Aristotle**	7. **Freud**
2. Plato	8. **Jakobson**
3. **Saussure**	9. Bateson
4. Chomsky	10. **Sapir**
5. Kant	11. **Peirce**
6. **Barthes**	12. **Lévi-Strauss**

Learning Aids

I also provide a brief biography of each author in the back of the book and questions for each selection that point out some topics that warrant attention as far as discussion, analysis of important ideas in the reading, and further research are concerned. In a separate section in the back of the book, I include some learning activities that are based on one or more of the selections. These learning activities or learning "games" are meant to be "played" in small groups of three or four students. These aids are meant to help you, my readers, get the most out of this book.

I hope that you will enjoy this book and find it useful in gaining a better understanding of some of the more important aspects of the communication process and the role it plays in giving texts and the mass media the power and resonance they have.

Confessions of a Pop Culture Junkie

I've been writing about comic strips, television shows, jokes and other kinds of humor, wrestling, fast foods, popular culture, tourism, and the various processes involved in communication and the media for more than forty years. I find these topics endlessly fascinating. For no sooner have I written about one subject, such as video games, than something completely different, such as reality television, appears.

So there's no rest, and I am like the mythic hero Sisyphus, condemned through eternity to push a boulder up to the top of a mountain and never able to do so, for just as Sisyphus approaches the top, he loses control and the boulder slides back down to the bottom of the mountain. I never may get to the top of the hill, but pushing the boulder up as far as I get, and making sense of whatever it is I'm interested in (to the extent I can make sense of anything, that is), is a source of great pleasure.

1 Words and Communication

The language game is similar to other games in that it is structured by rules, which speakers unconsciously learn simply by belonging to a particular speech community.... By the age of four or so they have mastered most of the exceedingly complex and abstract structures of their native tongues. In only a few more years children possess the entire linguistic system that allows them to utter and to understand sentences they have not previously heard....

Language is both a system of grammar and a human behavior which can be analyzed according to theories of interaction, play, and games. It can also be viewed as a shared system of rules and conventions, mutually intelligible to all members of a particular community, yet a system which nevertheless offers freedom and creativity in its use....

A language is like a game played with a fixed number of pieces—phonemes—each one easily recognized by native speakers. This is true of every language, except that the pieces change from one language game to another. Linguists ... generally agree that the language game is played with the following 45 phoneme "pieces":

21 consonants
9 vowels
4 semivowels (y, w, r)
4 stresses
4 pitches
1 juncture (pause between words)
3 terminal contours (to end sentences)

These 45 phonemes used in English today represent the total sound resources by which speakers can create an infinity of utterances....

For the rest of his life the child will speak sentences he has never before heard, and when he thinks or reads, he will still literally talk to himself. He can never escape from speech. And from speech flow all the other hallmarks of our humanity: those arts, sciences, laws, morals, customs, political and economic systems, and religious faiths that collectively are known as "culture."

— Peter Farb, *Word Play: What Happens When People Talk* (New York: Bantam, 1974), 6, 9, 294, 10

Questions for Discussion and Further Research

1. What does it mean to say that language is a "game"?
2. If language is a game, does that mean that conversation, based on language, is a game?
3. What other definitions of language does Farb offer?
4. Defend the assertion that speech is the basis of "all the other hallmarks of our humanity."
5. What are the attributes of a game? What implications does language being a game have?

When we speak, Farb explains, though we may not be aware of what we are doing, we always are following rules, the way people do when they play games. Learning a language involves being able to follow a number of complicated rules that we acquire unconsciously and internalize. We may not be aware of all these rules, but the fact that we are guided by them is demonstrated when we recognize when someone has not used the rules correctly.

We learn our languages when we are children, Farb says, and by around one year of age, children generally can speak recognizable words. This is quite a remarkable accomplishment, as anyone who has tried to learn a new language as an adult can recognize. Words are made up of phonemes, a Greek term (which literally means "sound unit") for the smallest significant unit of *sound*. According to *The Random House Dictionary of the English Language*, the Unabridged Edition (1976), phonemes are "the basic units of sounds by which morphemes, words and sentences are represented."

The English language has several hundred thousand words, but all of these words are created, Farb says, out of just three dozen sounds—which are selected from the many different sounds of which the human voice is capable. Our languages enable us to speak to one another—using words—and convey information, feelings, and all kinds of other things. Falk discusses the importance of language and speech both to individuals and to society. He points out that once children master language, they can speak and create sentences they've never heard or seen. It is language that is the cornerstone of culture, and it is words and the rules that tell us how to use them that shape, in varying degrees, our sense of ourselves and of our place in the universe.

It is with words, then, that our adventure in understanding human communication, in all its complexities, begins. Peter Farb has pointed out the importance of language to humans and the role that words play in communication, which is of central importance in the development of culture and society. Whatever else we are, above all else we are communicating animals, and one of the most important ways we communicate with one another is through language and words.

When we are children we pick up the rules of language from our parents and the linguistic community in which we find ourselves. In some countries, where a number of different languages are spoken, it is not unusual for children to learn several different languages.

As Francisco Yus, a Spanish linguistics professor, reminds us:

When people talk to each other, what people literally code (i.e., "say") on most occasions undetermine (that is, is less informative) the thoughts that the speaker really intends to communicate with these words. Normally, hearers are constantly fixing the real meaning of utterances from the "skeleton," as it were, of the words encoded. Examples would be "this child has a temperature," or "it will take time to fix your ear," or "a war is a war," which are meaningless (or too obvious) unless the hearer adjusts (via inference) the absent noncoded information intended by the speaker. Even if the importance of words cannot be questioned nowadays, inference has been stressed as very important for successful communication. The theory which I follow, relevance theory, claims that we are biologically geared towards searching for the most relevant information in incoming information, and that we invariably do that, often unconsciously. We cannot but do that since there is a biological urge involved which had developed the same way as languages have become more and more complex. (Personal communication)

Yus suggests that when we converse we don't transmit as much information as we think we're "sending," but we're also geared toward making sense of whatever is transmitted due to our natural disposition to make what we hear relevant.

There's a wonderful scene in *Henry* IV Part I where Falstaff, one of Shakespeare's great comedic creations, speculates on language. Falstaff and Henry, the Prince of Wales, constantly make fun of one another. In one famous scene, Falstaff speculates about language and, in particular, the word *honor*.

PRINCE: Why, thou owest God a death. [Exit]

FALSTAFF: 'Tis not due yet. I would be loath to pay him before his day. What need I be so forward with him that calls not on me? Well, 'tis no matter; honor pricks me on. Yea, but how if honor prick me off when I come on? How then? Can honor set to a leg? No. Or an arm? No. Or take away the grief of a wound? No. Honor hath no skill in surgery then? No. What is honor? A word. What is that word honor? What is that honor? Air. A trim reckoning! Who hath it? He that died a Wednesday. Doth he feel it? No. Doth he hear it? No. 'Tis insensible then? Yea, to the dead. But will [it] not live with the living? No. Why? Detraction will not suffer it. Therefore I'll none of it. Honor is a mere scutcheon—and so ends my catechism.

Honor is a word, Falstaff argues, and a word is mere air. Who has honor? Dead people. So Falstaff decides, rationalizing and justifying his cowardice, that he'll have nothing to do with it. (A scutcheon, by the way, is a painted representation of a shield with a coat of arms.)

What's interesting to consider is that words, such as honor, democracy, God, patriotism, and freedom, have played important roles in history. And that is because these words, and many others like them, are connected to our basic values and beliefs, and in defense of these ideas, people are willing to fight those who attack these ideas and to risk their lives.

As Edward Sapir has pointed out in his essay "Conceptual Categories in Primitive Languages,"

> The relation between language and experience is often misunderstood. Language is not a more or less systematic inventory of the various items of experience which seem relevant to the individual, as is so often naively assumed, but is also a self-contained, creative symbolic organization, which not only refers to experience largely acquired without its help but actually defines experience for us by reason of its formal completeness and because of our unconscious projection of its implicit expectations into the field of experience.... Such categories as number, gender, case, tense, mode, voice, "aspect" and a host of others, many of which are not recognized . . . are, of course derivative of experience at last analysis, but, once abstracted from experience, they are systematically elaborated in language and are not so much discovered in experience as imposed upon it because of the tyrannical hold that linguistic form has upon our orientation in the world. (Hymes 1964, 128)

Language, Sapir argues, affects the way we interpret the world and provides us with certain categories of thought such as number and gender. This suggests that language has the power to shape our perceptions of the world and, by implication, that each language provides a somewhat different picture of the world to the people who speak that language. Another facet of this topic is covered later in chapter 6, the selection from Basil Bernstein on elaborated and restricted codes in language.

2 ▸ Signs and Semiotics

Language is a system of signs that express ideas, and is therefore comparable to a system of writing, the alphabet of deaf-mutes, symbolic rites, polite formulas, military signals, etc. But it is the most important of all these systems. *A science that studies the life of signs within society* is conceivable.... I shall call it *semiology* (from Greek, semeîon "sign"). Semiology would show what constitutes signs, what laws govern them.

The linguistic sign unites not a thing and its name, but a concept and a sound-image. The latter is not the material sound, a purely physical thing, but the psychological imprint of the sound, the impression that it makes on our senses.... I call the combination of a concept and a sound-image a sign, but in current usage the term generally designates only a sound-image, a word, for example (*arbor*, etc.). One tends to forget that *arbor* is called a sign only because it carries the concept "tree," with the result that the idea of the sensory part implies the idea of the whole.

Ambiguity would disappear if the three notions involved here were designated by three names, each suggesting and opposing the others. I propose to retain the word *sign* [signe] to designate the whole and to replace *concept* and *sound-image* respectively by *signified* [signifié] and *signifier* [signifiant]; the last two terms have the advantage of indicating the opposition that separates them from each other and from the whole of which they are parts....

It is understood then that concepts are purely differential and defined not by their positive content but negatively by the relationship with the other terms of the system. Their most precise characteristic is in being what the others are not.... Signs function, then, not through their intrinsic value but through their relative position.

— Ferdinand de Saussure, *Course in General Linguistics* (New York: McGraw-Hill), 1966, 16, 66–67, 117, 118

Questions for Discussion and Further Research

1. How does Saussure define a sign?
2. What is the relationship that exists between a signifier and a signified?
3. Explain Saussure's statement that "concepts are purely differential."
4. What does Saussure mean when he says "in language there are only differences"?
5. What is the difference between language, speech, and parole?
6. Is what you are wearing today language, speech, or parole? Explain your choice.

Ferdinand de Saussure, a Swiss linguist, is not generally well known, but he is one of the most influential thinkers of the twentieth century. He is one of the founders of a science known as semiology or semiotics, the science of signs. The term *semeion* means "sign," and what Saussure did was suggest how signs work.

He makes a distinction between language, which is, he asserts, to be thought of as a social institution, and speech, which cannot be classified. In addition to these two categories, language and speech, there is what individuals do, what he calls speaking. "Execution is always individual," he says, "and the individual is always its master; I shall call the executive side *speaking* [*parole*] (Saussure, 1966, 13).

Thus we end up with three categories, as the chart below shows.

Language	Speech	Speaking
Langue	Language	Parole
Social institution	Individual and social	Individual

Speaking requires at least two people, Saussure writes, in which concepts or mental facts that are associated with linguistic sounds (sound-images) are transferred from one person's brain to that of another.

As Francisco Yus points out,

Saussure's idea of communication has been labeled a "code model," according to which thoughts are encoded (packed in a box, as it were), sent away, and decoded (the box is collected) without much information loss. According to recent pragmatics, communication is not so straightforward and secure, but mainly inferential and hence open to misunderstandings or partial understandings. (Personal communication)

Language, Saussure has suggested, is a social institution, but it is a much different social institution from political, legal, and other institutions. In

Signs and Semiotics

recent years, the term *semiotics* has become more widely used than *semiology*, and I will adopt that convention henceforth, except when quoting Saussure. In his chapter "The Nature of the Linguistic Sign," Saussure offers his analysis of the role of signs in language. It is important to recognize, Saussure explains, that the relationship that exists between a signifier and a signified is arbitrary and based on convention. That is, the meaning we give to words is socially determined and can be changed. The definitions we find in a dictionary are based on usage and convention, and they change over the years. This is a crucial insight.

There is one other concept from Saussure that I would like to deal with—a concept as important as his analysis of signs being made of signifieds and signifiers, united like two sides of a piece of paper. Saussure explains that in language it is the relationship of concepts that determines meaning. In language, he asserts, we find a system of interdependent terms in which the value of any term is based on the presence of other terms.

The meaning of words, then, is based on the system (or sentence) in which they are found and in their being oppositions of other terms in the system. Words get their meaning, Saussure explains, not from their positive content but by being opposites of other words. Or, as he puts it, "In language there are only differences" (1966, 120), and the most important difference, for most practical purposes, is that of opposition. These notions explain why it is we tend to think in terms of opposites: rich and poor, happy and sad, large and small, and so on. One caution: Saussure is not talking about negations, such as happy and unhappy, but oppositions, such as happy and sad. To simplify matters greatly, we know what happy is because we know it is not sad, and vice versa.

If Saussure is correct, it is language that structures the way we think, and we make sense of the world by interpreting concepts in terms of the way they are different from opposing concepts. His ideas about signs apply not only to words but also to other phenomena such as facial expressions, body language, fashions, hair styles, and all kinds of other forms of communication. For example, a smile is a signifier, but what is its signified? Because the relationship between signifiers and signifieds is based on convention and is arbitrary, a smile can signify many different things: happiness, friendliness, scorn, and so on.

Semiotics tells us that we are always sending messages to other people and they are sending messages to us. But interpreting what these signs mean is a complicated matter.

3 When I Use a Word, Humpty Dumpty Said . . .

beg your pardon?" Alice said with a puzzled air.

"I'm not offended" said Humpty Dumpty.

"I mean, what *is* an un-birthday present?"

"A present given when it isn't your birthday, of course."

Alice considered a little. "I like birthday presents best," she said at last.

"You don't know what you're talking about!" cried Humpty Dumpty. "How many days are there in a year?"

"Three hundred and sixty-five," said Alice.

"And how many birthdays have you?"

"One."

"And if you take one from three hundred and sixty-five, what remains?"

"Three hundred and sixty-four."

" . . . there are three hundred and sixty-four days when you might get un-birthday presents."

"Certainly," said Alice.

"And only one for birthday presents, you know. There's glory for you!"

"I don't know what you mean by 'glory,'" Alice said.

Humpty Dumpty smiled contemptuously. "Of course you don't—till I tell you. I meant 'there's a nice knock-down argument for you!'"

"But 'glory' doesn't mean 'a nice knock-down argument,'" Alice objected.

"When *I* use a word," Humpty Dumpty said, in a rather scornful tone, "It means just what I choose it to mean—neither more nor less."

"The question is," said Alice, "whether you can make words mean so many different things."

"The question is," said Humpty Dumpty, "which is to be master—that's all."

— Lewis Carroll, *Alice in Wonderland and Other Favorites* (New York: Pocket Books, 1951), 189–190

Questions for Discussion and Further Research

1. Would it be better to celebrate "unbirthdays" rather than birthdays? If so, why? If not, why not?
2. Was Humpty Dumpty correct when he asserted that words mean whatever he wants them to mean?
3. What is the difference between connotation and denotation?
4. Are the dictionary makers "masters" of what words mean? Defend your answer.
5. If words could mean whatever we wanted them to mean, could we communicate with others?

This discussion between Alice (of *Alice in Wonderland* fame) and Humpty Dumpty (who, as we all know, had a great fall and couldn't be put together again) raises an important question: What do words mean? Humpty Dumpty says that words mean whatever he wants them to mean. If people are to communicate with language, words have to mean the same thing to everyone, though words can have a number of different definitions, and the meanings and sense people have of words change over the years.

What is important to recognize is that the meanings of words are based on convention and are not natural or written in stone, so to speak. Dictionaries are assembled by taking the way words are conventionally used for their definitions. In more technical terms, we can recall Saussure's notion that a sign is composed of a signifier (in this case, a word) and a signified (its meaning or definition) and the relation between the two is arbitrary, that is, based on convention.

If you look in a good dictionary, you find that a word can have many different definitions: a preferred meaning, generally given first, but then a number of other meanings—generally similar in nature to the first meaning, but not always so. And definitions change over the years and new words come into existence (think of all the new words that came with the digital revolution),

which explains why dictionary makers are obliged to issue new editions of their dictionaries.

Our choice of words is very important. That's because words have different connotations and give readers a different sense of what an author means. Humpty Dumpty asked, Who is to be the master? The answer is—the people, whose definitions of terms are collected by dictionary makers.

Antithetical Meanings of Words

In my *Traumdeutung* I made a statement concerning one of the findings of my analytic work which I did not then understand. I will repeat it at the beginning of this review:

"The attitude of dreams towards the category of antithesis and contradiction is most striking. This category is simply ignored; the word 'No' does not seem to exist for a dream. Dreams show a special tendency to reduce two opposites to a unity or to represent them as one thing. Dreams even take the liberty, moreover, of representing any one element whatever by the opposite wish, so that it is at first impossible to ascertain, in regard to any element capable of an opposite, whether it is to be taken negatively or positively in the dream-thoughts. . . ."

To the chance reading of a work by the philologist K. Abel I owe my first understanding of the strange tendency of the dream-work to disregard negation and to express contraries by identical means of representation. . . . Abel continues, "Now in the Egyptian language, this unique relic of a primitive world, we find a fair number of words with two meanings, one of which says the exact opposite of the other."

The riddle is more easily solved than appears. Our conceptions always arise through comparison. "Were it always light we should not distinguish between light and dark, and accordingly could not have either the conception of, nor the word for, light. . . . It is clear that everything on this planet is relative and has independent existence only insofar as it is distinguished in its relations to and from other things."

— Sigmund Freud, "The Antithetical Sense of Primal Words."
A review of a pamphlet by Karl Abel, *Uber den Gegensinn der Urworte, 1884.* In S. Freud, *Character and Culture,* ed. Philip Rieff, 44–51 (New York: Collier Books, 1963)

Questions for Discussion and Further Research

1. Why does Freud assert that "no" doesn't exist in dreams?
2. How can a word have two meanings that are the opposites of one another?
3. Freud says "our conceptions arise through comparisons." Is that what Saussure argued?
4. Do you think the iceberg model does justice to Freud's theories on the unconscious?
5. What is meant by "reaction formation"?
6. Are most people in the United States dominated by their ids or super-egos? Defend your answer.
7. When is a cigar only a cigar?

Sigmund Freud considered his book *The Interpretation of Dreams* to be his most important work. Freud was born in Moravia in 1856 and died in London in 1939. He is considered the father of psychoanalytic theory and is generally considered one of the most important thinkers of the nineteenth and twentieth centuries, whose ideas have profoundly affected our ideas about culture and personality. At the core of his thinking is the notion that there are three levels of consciousness, which can be represented graphically by an iceberg. The part of the iceberg that we can see represents consciousness. There is a small portion of iceberg below the water that we can make out, and this represents pre-consciousness, material that we are not aware of but that we can bring to consciousness. The rest of the iceberg, about 90 percent, is buried in darkness, and this represents the unconscious—material that is not accessible to us, but which is nevertheless in our minds. What is important about the unconscious is that it plays an important role in shaping our behavior. Many of the things we do, Freud suggests, are shaped by unconscious imperatives—a power within us that we are not aware of and that we cannot control.

Freud also suggests that there are three forces operating in the human psyche: the id, which represents lust and desire; the superego, which represents conscience and guilt; and the ego, which tries to mediate between these two forces. All of these processes are unconscious. In his book on dreams, Freud deals with various processes that go on in dream work that serve to mask our true intentions.

Our dreams often have sexual content, but if this were expressed overtly, the dream would cause alarm in the superego and wake us; therefore, in dreams we use subterfuge and mask sexual content by displacement and condensation. In displacement we use substitute symbols (sticks, knives, etc., for the male genitals, and gardens, flowers, etc., for the female genitals) to avoid alarming the superego. In condensation, we combine things to mask their sexual content (one person's face, another person's body, a third person's clothes).

Freud writes about dreams representing ideas by their opposites, which calls to mind his theory about a defense mechanism he called *reaction formation.* According to this theory, we often express one feeling, such as hate, curiously, by adopting its opposite feeling, love. This happens generally when we have ambivalent attitudes toward someone; we suppress one side of our feelings and express the opposite one. Thus, we can act loving toward someone we hate and hateful toward someone we love.

Freud is struck by the way language shapes our thinking and the role that comparisons play in the way we make sense of the world. "Our conceptions always arise through comparisons," a statement very similar, in nature, to Saussure's idea that "in language there are only differences" (1966, 120, originally published in 1815). It's rather striking to notice that both Freud and Saussure, writing about the same time, have the same notion of the importance of language and of comparisons and differences. When Freud writes that "everything on this planet is relative and has independent existence only insofar as it is distinguished in its relations to and from other things," he is restating, in his own words, one of the basic notions of semiotics, as explained by Saussure. As Saussure reminds us, "Signs function, then, not through their intrinsic value but through their relative position" (1966, 118).

Every generation concludes that "Freud is finished," but his influence continues and his ideas about culture continue to play an important role in the thinking of many scholars and in the general climate of thought and opinion. Freud's ideas about the sexual content of symbols and phenomena such as castration anxiety and penis envy strike many people as far-fetched and absurd, as does his notion that infantile sexuality and, in particular, the Oedipus complex play an all-important role in our development and in our neuroses. Many feminist thinkers are outraged by his question "What do women want?"

Whatever you may think of Freud, the fact is that many of the terms he used continue to be used, and his thinking has shaped not only the work of countless therapists but of scholars in many different disciplines. Thus we have psychoanalytically inclined literary critics, anthropologists, political scientists, and culture theorists. Freud said "sometimes a cigar is only a cigar," indicating that cigars aren't always phallic symbols. But we must consider the other side of that comment, which suggests that sometimes a cigar *isn't* only a cigar.

5 ▸ Society Precedes the Individual

For human beings, society is the primary reality, not just the sum of individual activities, nor the contingent manifestations of Mind; and if one wishes to study human behavior, one must grant that there is a social reality.... In short, sociology, linguistics, and psychoanalytic psychology are possible only when one takes the meanings which are attached to and which differentiate objects and actions in society as a primary reality, as facts to be explained. And since meanings are a social product, explanation must be carried out in social terms. It is as if Saussure, Freud, and Durkheim had asked, "What makes individual experience possible? What enables men and women to operate with meaningful objects and actions? What enables them to communicate and act meaningfully?" And the answer they postulated was social which, though formed by human activities, are the conditions of experience. To understand individual experience one must study the social norms which make it possible.... Saussure, Freud, and Durkheim thus reverse the perspective which makes society the result of individual behavior and insist that behavior is made possible by collective social systems individuals have assimilated, consciously or unconsciously.

Since human beings make noises, use gestures, employ combinations of objects or actions in order to convey meaning, there is a place for a discipline which would analyze this kind of activity and make explicit the systems of convention on which it rests.... Semiotics is thus based on the assumption that insofar as human actions or productions convey meaning, insofar as they function as signs, there must be an underlying system of conventions and distinctions which makes this meaning possible. Where there are signs there is system.

— Jonathan Culler, *Ferdinand de Saussure,* rev. ed. (Ithaca, NY: Cornell University Press, 1986), 86, 87, 106

Questions for Discussion and Further Research

1. What does Culler mean when he says "society is the primary reality"?
2. How can society "precede" the individual? Is this a chicken and egg argument?
3. Why isn't society the result of individual behavior?
4. What is the underlying basis of the science of semiotics for Culler?
5. Is it correct to say that the single individual doesn't think? Explain why or why not.
6. Why is the notion of the "self-made man/woman" an illusion? What does de Tocqueville say?

Culler raises an important point. If signs are to be meaningful, there must be a society that, one way or another, teaches people how signs are to be interpreted. The meanings of signs are not natural but determined by society. Individual behavior, Culler argues, is the result of there being something we call society, and individuals are not the creators of society. Margaret Thatcher, former prime minister of England, argued that society is just an abstraction and only individuals exist. Culler turns this argument on its head and suggests that you need society for individuals to exist—to learn how to speak a language and to learn what signs mean. That is, we are social animals and must not forget the role society plays in our lives.

The idea that only individuals exist is not something we are born with; we learn it from society. In a classic work of sociological analysis, *Ideology and Utopia*, Karl Mannheim writes,

> Strictly speaking it is incorrect to say that the single individual thinks. Rather it is more correct to insist that he participates in thinking further what other men have thought before him. He finds himself in an inherited situation with patterns of thought which are appropriate to this situation and attempts to elaborate further the inherited modes of response or to substitute others for them in order to deal more adequately with the new challenges which have arisen out of shifts and changes in his situation. Every individual is therefore in a two-fold sense predetermined by the fact of growing up in a society: on the one hand he finds a ready-made situation and on the other he finds in that situation preformed patterns of thought and conduct. The persons who talk most about human freedom are those who are actually most blindly subject to social determination. (Mannheim 1936, 3)

Mannheim's book is one of the most fundamental statements in the sociology of knowledge—that branch of sociology that investigates the role of social determinants of knowledge and behavior. He argued that we must "uncover unconscious motivations in order to make those forces which formerly ruled them into objects of conscious rational decision" (1936, 48).

This theory draws upon the ideas of the great French sociologist Emile Durkheim, who argued that there is a complex relationship between individuals and society: individuals are in society and society is in individuals. That is, we may be individuals with certain ideas and notions and tastes but these all come from society, and it is just as fallacious to suggest that only individuals exist as it is to suggest that individuals are completely socially determined. Alexis de Tocqueville coined the term *individualism* in *Democracy in America*. As he explained, "Individualism proceeds from erroneous judgment more than from depraved feelings; it originates as much in deficiencies of mind as in perversity of heart" (1956, 193). He argued that the egalitarian nature of American society tended to make people forget about or downplay the importance of social institutions.

Culler points out that Saussure, Freud, and Durkheim stress the importance of society in making communication possible and in shaping individuals. Each person may be distinctive and have unique qualities of mind and temperament, but we achieve our distinctiveness, it can be argued, by assembling in different ways the possibilities that society provides to us. Thus, the idea of the "self-made" man or woman, completely independent of society, is an illusion (that is, false notion) that we learn from the only place we can learn it—from society.

From a semiotic perspective, if signs are to have meaning, there has to be "an underlying system of conventions which makes this meaning possible." As Saussure reminds us, semiotics is "a science that studies the life of signs within society" (1966, 16). If there are to be signs that can be understood, there must be society to teach us what those signs mean.

6 Language Codes

I shall argue that forms of socialization orient the child towards speech codes which control access to relatively context-tied or relatively context-independent meanings. Thus I shall argue that elaborated codes orient their users towards universalistic meanings, whereas restricted codes orient, sensitize, their users to particularistic meanings: that the linguistic-realization of the two orders are different, and so are the social relationships which realize them. Elaborated codes are less tied to a given or local structure and thus contain the potentiality of change in principles.

In the case of elaborated codes the speech is freed from its evoking social structure and *takes* on an autonomy. A university is a place organized around talk. Restricted codes are more tied to a local social structure and have a reduced potential for disuse in principles. Where codes are elaborated, the socialized has more access to the grounds of his own socialization, and so can enter into a reflexive relationship to the social order he has taken over. Where codes are restricted, the socialized has less access to the grounds of his socialization, and thus reflexiveness may be limited in range. One of the effects of the class system is to limit access to elaborated codes.

I shall go on to suggest that restricted codes have their basis in condensed symbols whereas elaborated codes have their basis in articulated symbols. That restricted codes draw upon metaphor whereas elaborated codes draw upon rationality. That these codes constrain the contextual use of language in critical socializing contexts and in this way regulate the orders of relevance and relations which the socialized takes over. From this point of view, change in habitual speech codes involves changes in the means by which object and person relationships are realized.

— Basil Bernstein, "Social Class, Language and Socialization," in *Language and Social Context,* ed. Pier Paolo Giglioli, 157–178 (Harmondsworth, England: Penguin, 1972), 164

Questions for Discussion and Further Research

1. How do restricted and elaborated codes affect people's lives?
2. What are the basic characteristics of restricted and elaborated codes?
3. What positive attributes are connected to each code?
4. How do language codes shape future behavior?
5. Does this coding notion help explain the "culture of poverty"?
6. Which code did your parents speak when you grew up? Give examples.
7. Do you think the mass media have affected the codes people learn?

Basil Bernstein's theories about restricted and elaborated codes in the speech of different classes of people is highly controversial. His argument, in brief, is that there is a difference in the way middle- and upper-class English people speak to their children from the way working class people speak to their children, and that these two "codes" have important effects on the way children develop and think about their possibilities. In his other writings on language, he suggests that these two codes are different in the following manner:

Elaborated code	Restricted code
Complex grammar	Simple grammar
Vocabulary is varied	Vocabulary is uniform
Sentence structure complex	Sentence structure simple
High level of conceptualization	Low level of conceptualization
Use of qualifiers common	Little use of qualifiers
Logical	Emotional
Users aware of code	Users unaware of code
Meaning elaborated verbally	Context shapes meaning
Middle classes	Working classes

What is important to recognize is that the code children learn becomes a prism or matrix through which they interpret the world and ascertain their place in it. Both kinds of codes have strong points and weak points, but the restricted code, it is implied, gives working-class children a much more limited sense of possibility.

What Bernstein's work suggests is that the "coding" we are subjected to, as we grow up, helps shape our behavior. For example, if we learn a code that has a low level of conceptualization and few qualifiers, we may end up with a rather simplistic perspective on things and with a kind of present-mindedness that precludes long-range thinking—about the value of higher education, for example. This mindset makes it very difficult for middle-class (elaborated code) social workers to deal with people "locked" into the culture of poverty. That is because, in part, they speak differently coded versions of their language.

The Structuralist Perspective

We cannot read much of Lévi-Strauss without a feeling of excitement. . . . He has developed most explicitly in connection with myth his ideas of the place of sociology within a single grand discipline of Communication. This part of his teaching draws very broadly on the structural analysis of linguistics, and on cybernetics and communication theory in general, and to some extent on the related theory of games. Briefly, its starting-point is that it is the nature of the mind to work through form. Any experience is received in a structured form, and these forms or structures, which are a condition of knowing, are generally unconscious (as, for example, the unconscious categories of knowledge). Furthermore, they vary little in modern or ancient times. They always consist in the creation of pairs of opposites, which are balanced against one another and built up in various (algebraically representable) ways. All the different kinds of patterned activity can be analyzed according to the different structures they produce. For example, social life is a matter of interaction between persons. There are three different types of social communication. First, there is kinship, the structure underlying the rules for transferring women; second, there is the economy, that is the structure underlying transfer of goods and services; third, there is the underlying structure of language. The promise is that if we can get at these structures, display and compare them, the way is open for a true science of society. . . .

Lévi-Strauss recognizes that its [myth's] structures belong to a different level of mental activity from those of language and the technique must be correspondingly different. . . . It assumes that the analysis of myth should proceed like the analysis of language. In both language and myth the separate units have no meaning by themselves, they acquire it only because of the way in which they are assembled.

— Mary Douglas, *Implicit Meanings: Essays in Anthropology* (London: Routledge & Kegan Paul, 1975), 153–154

Questions for Discussion and Further Research

1. What does it mean to say "the mind works through form"?
2. Claude Lévi-Strauss believes the way the mind works hasn't changed over history. What do you think?
3. What is the role of paired opposites in the ideas of Lévi-Strauss?
4. Why do "separate units" have no meaning in language?
5. It is the way that myths are assembled that is crucial, Douglas asserts. Why?
6. Define structuralism and explain its significance.

Mary Douglas is one of the most important social anthropologists of recent years. Her discussion of the ideas of Claude Lévi-Strauss, whom we will read next, provides an important insight that is related to the discussions that have preceded this chapter. Once again we are dealing with language, and once again the point is made that meaning is relational—that, to put matters simply, the meaning of a term stems from its place in a sentence, and the meaning of anything is dependent upon the context in which we find it. The way language seems to work, it is suggested, is by establishing "pairs of opposites," as Douglas puts it. Freud reminded us of the same thing: If there's no dark, the concept of light becomes meaningless. If there's no "rich," then there's no "poor."

Lévi-Strauss is identified with a perspective called structuralism, which analyzes phenomena in terms of their basic units and the way these units are assembled. The relations between elements in anything are of fundamental interest. Just as Freud argues that our unconscious shapes our behavior, the structuralists argue that the relationship between elements in something like a myth, which we are unaware of, is what is of crucial significance. If we can get at these underlying structures and examine them, we can better understand the way we think and the way we act. As Jacques Ehrmann writes in his introduction to a book he edited, *Structuralism*,

> Structuralism attempts to uncover the internal relationships which give different languages . . . their form and function. On a broader view, scholars are now trying to lay the bases for a science of signs—semiotics—which would include not only these languages but also any system of signs. (Ehrmann 1970, ix)

According to Mary Douglas, the mind works in certain ways—through form—and it is semiotics and its allied field of structuralism, as exemplified in the work of Lévi-Strauss, that best enables us to understand these forms and the rules and binary oppositions that shape our understanding of life. His influence has waned since the eighties, and we are now in what some call a "poststructuralist era" in the social sciences.

The Structuralist Perspective

8 Culture and the Unconscious

The principle that anthropology draws its originality from the unconscious nature of collective phenomena stems (though in a still obscure and ambiguous manner) from a statement made by Tyler. Having defined anthropology as the study of "Culture or Civilization," he described culture as "that complex whole which includes knowledge, belief, art, morals, law, custom, and any other capabilities and habits acquired by man as a member of society." ... There is rarely any doubt that the unconscious reasons for practicing a custom or sharing a belief are remote from the reasons given to justify them. Even in our own society, table manners, social etiquette, fashions of dress, and many of our moral, political, and religious attitudes are scrupulously observed by everyone, although their real origin and function are not often critically examined. ...

Boas must be given credit for defining the unconscious nature of cultural phenomena with admirable lucidity. By comparing cultural phenomena to language from this point of view, he anticipated both the subsequent development of linguistic theory and a future for anthropology whose rich promise we are just beginning to perceive. He showed that the structure of language remains unknown to the speaker until the introduction of a scientific grammar. Even then the language continues to mold discourse beyond the consciousness of the individual, imposing on his thought conceptual schemes which are taken as objective categories. ...

If, as we believe to be the case, the unconscious activity of the mind consists of imposing form upon content, and if these forms are fundamentally the same for all minds—ancient and modern, primitive and civilized (as the study of the symbolic function, expressed in language, so strikingly indicates)—it is necessary and sufficient to grasp the unconscious structure underlying each institution and each custom, in order to obtain a principle of interpretation valid for other institutions and other customs. ...

— Claude Lévi-Strauss, *Structural Anthropology* (Garden City, NY: Anchor, 1967), 19–22

Questions for Discussion and Further Research

1. How did E. B. Tyler define culture?
2. What changes would you make to this definition? How do you define culture?
3. If the unconscious imposes form on content, how do we know this?
4. Why does Lévi-Strauss argue that the forms imposed by the mind are universal?
5. How can these forms be the same for all minds, ancient and modern, primitive and civilized?
6. How can collective phenomena be unconscious? What aspects of life are covered by this notion?

Lévi-Strauss, like so many of the other thinkers dealt with in this book, stresses the importance of the unconscious elements in the human psyche. If we all knew why we did everything we did, then there would be no need for social sciences. It is because we are either blind to the unconscious imperatives operating in our psyches and our behavior, or because we refuse to recognize the reasons why we do things, that we need social scientists to probe beneath the surface of things and find out why we dress in certain ways, eat certain things, adopt certain table manners, watch the television shows we watch, and do all kinds of other things.

The great anthropologist Franz Boas showed that people don't recognize the way their languages work until someone writes a grammar for the language. We learn to speak by listening to our parents, our siblings, our playmates, and others, and by osmosis, so it seems, we learn the rules for speaking, though we aren't aware of them, that are considered correct. And we learn accents, too. I, for example, was raised in Boston and thus I do not pronounce "r" sounds. I say "pahk your cah in Hahvahd yahd" instead of "park your car in Harvard yard."

What is important to recognize, Lévi-Strauss asserts, is that people unconsciously impose form upon content and, it can be assumed, Lévi-Strauss suggested, that these forms are "fundamentally the same for all minds—ancient and modern, primitive and civilized." This means that there are unconscious structures in all our institutions in all societies and cultures that a perceptive anthropologist can discover, if the analysis is carried far enough. The anthropologist uses human consciousness to discover what is hidden in the unconscious and focuses attention on the relationships that exist between elements, of all kinds, in a system.

Culture and the Unconscious

9 ▸ The Importance of Metaphor

Metaphor is for most people a device of the poetic imagination and the rhetorical flourish—a matter of extraordinary rather than ordinary language. Moreover, metaphor is typically viewed as a characteristic of language alone, a matter of words rather than thought or action. For this reason, most people think they can get along perfectly well without metaphor. We have found, on the contrary, that metaphor is pervasive in everyday life, not just in language but in thought and action. Our ordinary conceptual system, in terms of which we both think and act, is fundamentally metaphoric in nature. The concepts that govern our thought are not just matters of the intellect. They also govern our everyday functioning, down to the most mundane details. Our concepts structure what we perceive, how we get around in the world, and how we relate to other people. Our conceptual system thus plays a central role in defining our everyday realities. If we are right in suggesting that our conceptual system is largely metaphorical, what we experience and what we do every day is very much a matter of metaphor.

— George Lakoff and Mark Johnson, *Metaphors We Live By* (Chicago: University of Chicago Press, 1980), 3

Questions for Discussion and Further Research

1. Define the following terms: metaphor, simile, metonymy, synecdoche.
2. Defend or attack the notion that our conceptual system is fundamentally metaphoric.
3. Give some examples of how metaphors may affect everyday behavior.
4. What is a concept? How do concepts affect our behavior?
5. How can a snake be both metaphoric and metonymic?
6. Discuss the implications of specific metaphors. Find ones that are interesting.

Our authors raise a very important point—namely that much of our thinking, though we may not be aware of the fact—is metaphoric in nature. Along with metaphor, there is another concept that plays an important role in the way we think—metonymy. Metaphor is based on analogy and similarity; we talk about one thing in terms of another. "My love is a rose." A weaker form of analogy, a simile, uses "like" or "as." "My love is like a rose."

Metonymy, on the other hand, is based upon association. We learn, as we grow up in a particular society, to associate certain things with other things. For example, because a Rolls Royce automobile costs an enormous amount of money, we learn to associate a Rolls Royce with wealth and with a certain kind of person. Though a Rolls Royce and a Ferrari each cost a great deal of money, we think of Ferrari drivers as being different—perhaps younger and more sporty—than owners of Rolls Royce automobiles. A form of metonymy in which a part is used to stand for the whole, or the whole for a part, is called synecdoche. Thus, for example, we often use the Pentagon to stand for the entire military establishment or use the term "wheels" to stand for a car, as in "I've got new wheels."

These four kinds of speech play an enormous role in our thinking:

Term	Process	Strength	Example
Metaphor	Analogy	Strong	My love is a rose
Simile	Analogy	Weak	My love is like a rose
Metonymy	Association	Strong	Rolls Royce implies wealth
Synecdoche	Association	Weak	I've got new wheels

The media make great use of these methods of thinking. It's much easier to show an image of someone in a Rolls Royce to suggest wealth than it is to use language to explain the relationship. An image can be both metaphoric and metonymic at the same time.

The Importance of Metaphor

Consider a text in which there is a snake. You often see snakes in horror films. Snakes are conventionally understood to be phallic symbols, so the implied metaphor is "a snake is a penis." Or if you think that is too strong, you can think of the simile "a snake is like a penis." There is also the metonymic connection that is important. Snakes, especially in a paradisical setting, suggest the story of the Garden of Eden. It was there that a snake talked to Eve, who then convinced Adam to eat from the tree of knowledge, against God's commandment. This led God to expel Adam and Eve from the Garden of Eden. So an image of a snake, in certain situations, can generate a number of significant ideas in our minds—some of which we may not be conscious of. But that doesn't mean we aren't affected by them.

There is another aspect to metaphor that should be considered. Metaphors often have implications that are very important. They shape our notions about what we can expect, so they play a much more important part in our lives than we might imagine. Certain ideas are logically connected with a particular metaphor, and we must learn to be aware of the logical implications of metaphors that we accept as correct. These terms, metaphor and metonymy, were given prominence in an important article by Roman Jakobson on aphasia, an affliction involving speech caused by brain damage. Jakobson was one of the most important linguists of the twentieth century. It is to his model of the communication process that we now turn.

A Model of the Communication Process

L anguage must be investigated in all the variety of its functions.... An out-
line of these functions demands a concise survey of the constitutive
factors in any speech event, in any act of verbal communication. The
ADDRESSER sends a MESSAGE to the ADDRESSEE. To be operative the
message requires a CONTEXT referred to ("referent" in another, somewhat
ambiguous nomenclature), seizable by the addressee, and either verbal or
capable of being verbalized; a CODE fully, or at least partially, common to the
addresser and addressee (or in other words, to the encoder and decoder of the
message); and finally, a CONTACT, a physical channel and psychological connection between the addresser and addressee, enabling both of them to enter
and stay in communication. All these factors inalienably involved in verbal
communication may be schematized as follows:

```
┌─────────────────────────────────────────────────┐
│                    CONTEXT                        │
│                                                   │
│   ADDRESSER     MESSAGE     ADDRESSEE             │
│   ─────────────────────────────────────          │
│                                                   │
│                    CONTACT                        │
│                                                   │
│                     CODE                          │
└─────────────────────────────────────────────────┘
```

Each of these six factors determines a different function of language.
Although we distinguish six basic aspects of language, we could, however, hardly
find verbal messages that would fulfill only one function.... The verbal structure
of a message depends primarily on the predominant function. But even though
... an orientation toward the CONTEXT—briefly the so-called REFERENTIAL,
"denotative," "cognitive," function—is the leading task of numerous messages, the
accessory participation of the other functions in such messages must be taken
into account by the observant linguist.

The so-called EMOTIVE or "expressive" function, focused on the AD-
DRESSER, aims a direct expression of the speaker's attitude toward what he is speaking about.... There are messages primarily to establish, to prolong, or to discontinue
communication, to check whether the channel works ("Hello, do you hear me?"), to
attract the attention of the interlocutor or to confirm his continued attention.

— Roman Jakobson, "Linguistics and Poetics," in *Modern Criticism and
Theory: A Reader*, ed. David Lodge (New York: Longman, 1988), 34

Questions for Discussion and Further Research

1. List and define Jakobson's six constitutive factors involved in verbal communication.
2. Define and explain the difference between "emotive" and "referential" functions.
3. Scholes says there is a difference between a message and a meaning. Explain.
4. How do the different codes people have cause problems for the mass media?

In his book, *Structuralism in Literature: An Introduction*, Robert Scholes discusses Jakobson's model of communication. Scholes writes,

> Whether we are considering ordinary conversation, a public speech, a letter, or a poem, we always find a *message* which proceeds from a *sender* to a *receiver*. These are the most obvious aspects of communication. But a successful communication depends on three other aspects of the event as well: the message must be delivered through a *contact*, physical and/or psychological; it must be framed in a *code*; and it must refer to a *context*. In the area of context, we find what a message is about. But to get there we must understand the code in which the message is framed—as in the present case, my messages reach you through the medium of an academic/literary subcode of the English language. (1974, 24)

He adds that even if we know the code, we still must receive the message. What the message does is unite a sender and a receiver, but he points out that we cannot assume that the message is the same as the meaning. Someone must interpret the meaning of a message.

This is a big problem with the mass media, in which the codes of the senders are often different from the codes of the receivers. In many cases, the receivers don't realize that they are decoding a message (an advertisement, something someone says in a sitcom, and so on) differently from the way the sender envisioned they would. We must also recognize, as Jakobson points out, that the context of a message is very important. Consider, for example, the difference the phrase "pass me the hypodermic needle" makes if is spoken in a dark alley (context 1) as contrasted to a hospital (context 2).

Let me offer a chart that amplifies the one offered by Jakobson on the six "aspects" of language:

Addresser	Sender of message
Message	Content sent
Addressee	Receiver of message
Context	Circumstances in which message is given
Contact	Channel in which message is sent
Code	Understood by both addresser and addressee
	(Example: English language being used in this book)

These are, Jakobson suggests, the fundamental units of the communication process. When we deal with audiovisual communication such as television, we must factor in other elements—facial expression, body language, music, lighting, editing, sound effect, and the way actors say their lines—all of which further complicate our decoding of messages.

Jakobson also deals with some functions of language that, he explains, can be referential, focusing on the denotative or cognitive qualities of a message, or emotive, focusing on the addresser's attitudes about what is being communicated. He deals with other functions that need not be discussed here. The Jakobson model of communication is only one of a number of different models—each of which attempts to best represent the communication process and explain its effects.

11 ▸ The Lasswell Formula

A convenient way to describe an act of communication is to answer the following questions:

Who?
Says what?
In which channel?
To whom?
With what effect?

— Harold Lasswell, "The Structure and Function of Communication in Society," in *The Communication of Ideas,* ed. Lyman Bryson (New York: Harper & Brothers, 1948), 37–51

Questions for Discussion and Further Research

1. What is a formula? Is it different from a model? If so, how?
2. What is the Lasswell formula? How does it relate to Jakobson's model?
3. Some communications scholars have attacked it. Why did they do so?
4. Define "phatic" communication and give some examples of it.

This brief statement is known as the Lasswell formula and has been widely discussed, debated, and critiqued by communication theorists since it was first published. A formula, for our purposes, can be defined as a statement expressing some fundamental truth or principle. It often has a mathematical nature, but not always. In the chart below, I show how the Lasswell formula is related to Jakobson's model of the communication process, which was dealt with in the previous chapter. We find the following elements in these two approaches:

Lasswell	Jakobson
Who?	An addresser or sender of a message
Says what?	The message or content
In which channel	The medium or contact
To whom?	The addressee or receiver of the message
With what effect?	The functions of the message

Models can be defined as abstract representations of processes that occur in the world, and as such, they have their values and their limitations. One value they have is that they generally can be represented graphically and thus give people an easy-to-understand overview of whatever the model is describing. One limitation they have is that they tend to simplify complicated matters and often leave out important considerations.

The Lasswell formula assumes that communication is always based on influencing receivers and thus having certain desired effects. This is highly questionable, for though a great deal of communication is created to have certain effects—think, for example of advertising—there is also some communication that is not based on persuasion. There is what is known as phatic communication that is used to express emotions rather than communicate information. Think, for example, of the way men grunt in gyms when they are lifting weights. Is that meant to influence and persuade others? And when communication does have effects, researchers have been divided, for many years, about whether the effects are powerful and long lasting or short and trivial. Discussions relating to the effects of communication and the mass media are found throughout this book.

12 Art and Society: A Model

Four elements in the total situation of a work of art are discriminated and made salient, by one or another synonym, in almost all theories which aim to be comprehensive. First, there is the *work,* the artistic product itself. And since this is a human product, an artifact, the second common element is the artificer, the *artist.* Third, the work is taken to have a subject, which directly or deviously, is derived from existing things—to be about, or signify, or reflect something which either is or bears some relation to an objective state of affairs. This third element, whether held to consist of people and actions, ideas and feelings, material things and events, or super-sensible essences, has frequently been denoted by that word-of-all-work, "nature"; but let us use the more neutral and comprehensive term, *universe,* instead. For the final element we have the *audience,* the listeners, spectators, or readers to whom the work is addressed, or to whose attention, at any rate, it becomes available.

On this framework of artist, work, universe, and audience I wish to spread out various theories for comparison. To emphasize the artificiality of the device, and at the same time make it easier to visualize the analyses, let us arrange the four coordinates in a convenient pattern. A triangle will do, with the work of art, the thing to be explained, in the center.

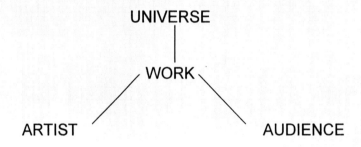

Although any reasonably adequate theory takes some account of all four elements, almost all theories, as we shall see, exhibit a discernible orientation toward one only.

— M. H. Abrams, *The Mirror and the Lamp: Romantic Theory and the Critical Tradition* (New York: Norton, 1958), 6

Questions for Discussion and Further Research

1. What are the four "coordinates" involving works of art for Abrams?
2. How does Abrams define each of these coordinates?
3. Abrams says most theories concentrate on only one coordinate. Why is this so?
4. What changes does the Berger model make to the Abrams model?
5. What did McLuhan mean when he said "the medium is the message"?

brams points out that most literary critics—to whom his book is primarily addressed—tend to focus on one of the four elements in his model, neglecting, it is implied, important considerations. Thus, for example, some literary scholars focus on the artist and write biographies that deal with the personality and life experiences of the writer and their impact on his or her work. Some critics focus on the work or text, often excluding (as in the case of the so-called new criticism of the fifties) everything else.

I have developed my own model of communication, as it involves the media, that was influenced by one proposed by M. H. Abrams, except that I add media to the mix and use *society* instead of *universe*. Actually, the way Abrams discusses this term, "people and actions" suggests the term *society*, and I have used it instead of *universe*, which is too broad to be of any use. I argue that there are five focal points that one can deal with in considering mass-mediated communication. To simplify matters and help my readers remember these focal points, I use terms that start with A—except for one, Medium.

Thus we find an Artist (sender, creator or group of creators), Art (the texts created, conveying a message), an Audience (those who receive the message), America (a society in which the message is created and disseminated), and a Medium (such as radio, television, film, books, and magazines). This model is shown below:

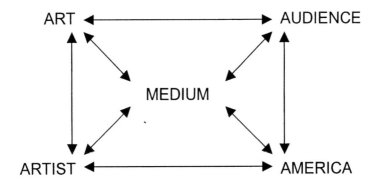

There are lines connecting each of these five focal points, indicating that they are all connected to one another and can influence one another. For example, the society in which artists/creators work has an impact on their work. What I didn't realize when I developed my model is that in many respects it parallels the Lasswell formula. A comparison of the three models follows:

Lasswell	Abrams	Berger
Who	Artist	Artist
Says what	Work	Artwork (text)
In which channel	N/A	Medium
To whom	Audience	Audience
With what effect?	Universe	America (society)

My model does not focus on the matter of effects directly, but the notion that communication has effects, of one sort or another, is more or less implied in my formulation. And it adds an element missing in the Abrams model, that of the Medium in which the work of art is created and communicated to others.

Marshall McLuhan, in one of his most famous and controversial statements, said "the medium is the message," which suggests that a medium is more important than the content it carries. I would not go that far, but I would assert that we must be mindful of the medium since it plays an important role in the way artists create and communicate their texts.

13 ▶ Dialogic Aspects of Communication

The word is born in a dialogue as a living rejoinder with it; the world is shaped in dialogic interaction with an alien word that is already in the object. A word forms a concept of its own object in a dialogic way. . . . The word in living conversation is directly, blatantly, oriented toward a future answer-word: it provokes an answer, anticipates it and structures itself in the answer's direction. Forming itself in an atmosphere of the already spoken, the word is at the same time determined by that which has not yet been said but which is needed and in fact anticipated by the answering world. Such is the case in any living dialogue.

The listener and his response are regularly taken into account when it comes to everyday dialogue and rhetoric, but every other sort of discourse as well is oriented toward an understanding that is "responsive"—although this orientation is not particularized in an independent act and is not compositionally marked. Responsive understanding is a fundamental force, one that participates in the formulation of discourse, and it is moreover an *active* understanding, one that discourse senses as resistance or support enriching the discourse. . . .

The linguistic significance of a given utterance is understood against the background of language, while its actual meaning is understood against the background of other concrete utterances on the same theme, a background made up of contradictory opinions, points of view and value judgments—that is, precisely that background that, as we see, complicates the path of any word toward its object. Only now this contradictory environment of alien words is present to the speaker not in the object, but rather in the consciousness of the listener.

— Michael Holquist, ed., *The Dialogic Imagination: Four Essays by M. M. Bakhtin,* trans. Caryl Emerson and Michael Holquist (Austin: University of Texas Press, 1981), 279–281

Questions for Discussion and Further Research

1. Why does Bakhtin assert that "the word is born in a dialogue"?
2. How does he define "dialogic"? Define "dialogism."
3. How does he explain the way we understand linguistic utterances?
4. Define "intertextuality." Give some examples of it from films, TV, and music.
5. Can a work ever not be intertextual? Defend your answer.
6. Communication must take cultural norms into account. How does this affect media?
7. Is there a difference between conversation and dialogue? Explain your answer.

Mikhail Bakhtin (1875–1975) was an influential theorist of communication from Russia who has been "rediscovered" in the past several decades. He elaborated a theory of language called "dialogism," wrote important works on Dostoevsky, and is probably most famous for his book *Rabelais and His World*. His theories have influenced many contemporary scholars in literature and cultural studies, who have used his ideas to explicate everything from humor to film and literature.

Dialogism focuses on the two-way aspects of communication—taking dialogue as its main metaphor for the communication process. It is an oversimplification to say that communication is dialogue, but not too far from the truth. Dialogue is basic to understanding communication, not monologue—in which we are talking to ourselves, so to speak. When we speak with others, we must keep in mind what has already been said and anticipate what will be said. And this property is true of all discourse, of all kinds of communication in all media. That is, communication must take into account cultural norms and beliefs and use them, just as it must consider future responses to that communication.

This dialogic perspective, which takes into account previous utterances and texts in all media, implies another of Bakhtin's theories, one known as intertextuality. What this says, in brief, is that there are strong relationships between texts being produced at any moment in time and other texts that were previously produced. In some cases, as in parody, we are conscious of these earlier texts, but in many other cases, artists in all media who are creating texts (movies, television shows, novels, songs, and so on) are not always conscious of the way these previously produced texts influence them—either stylistically or in terms of their content.

14 Conversation as Narrative

In *Poetics*, Aristotle said that a narrative has a beginning, middle, and end. Ever since, scholars agree that sequence is necessary, if not sufficient, for narrative.... Labov and Waletzsky (1967) argued that stories follow a chronicle sequence. The order of events moves in a linear way through time and the "order cannot be changed without changing the inferred sequence of events in the original semantic interpretation." A narrative, according to this definition, is always responding to the question "and then what happened?"...

In conversation, tellers sometimes let listeners know a story is coming and indicate when it is over, with entrance and exit talk.... "Once upon a time" and "they lived happily ever after" are classic examples in folktales of bracketing devices. But stories told in research interviews are rarely so clearly bounded, and locating them is often a complex interpretive process. Where one chooses to begin and end a narrative can profoundly alter its shape and meaning.

Like weight-bearing walls, personal narratives depend on certain structures to hold them together. Stories told in conversation share common parameters, although they may be put together in contrasting ways and, as a result, point to different interpretations. Events become meaningful because of their placement in a narrative.

Labov's ... structural approach is paradigmatic.... Narratives, he argues, have formal properties and each has a function. A "fully formed" one includes six common elements: an abstract (summary of the substance of the narrative), orientation (time, place, situation, participants), complicating action (sequence of events), evaluation (significance and meaning of the action, attitude of the narrator), resolution (what finally happened), and coda (returns the perspective to the present). With these structures, a teller constructs a story from a primary experience and interprets the significance of events in clauses and embedded evaluations.

— Catherine Kohler Riessman, *Narrative Analysis* (Thousand Oaks, CA: Sage Publications, 1993), 17–19

Questions for Discussion and Further Research

1. Discuss Labov's six rules and give examples from a conversation you've had.
2. Can the order of events in a conversation be changed without affecting the meaning? Explain.
3. How can a film or television story be considered a "glorified" conversation?
4. Does dialogue in films and other media narratives follow Labov's rules? Justify your answer.
5. Narratives are one way we make sense of the world. How does this work?
6. What implications does the importance of narratives have for the mass media?

What Riessman does in this selection is point out some of the rules we use when we converse. We probably are not aware of these rules in the sense that we have not articulated them and thought about them. We have, instead, picked them up subliminally, from our culture. Our conversations, she points out, are narratives—that is, stories—and as such, must obey certain rules and conventions if they are to be intelligible to our listeners. Let me list these rules to give them more focus. Our conversations usually contain the following items:

1. An *abstract*—that is, giving an overview of our story.
2. An *orientation*—telling us the who, what, where, when, and why of the story.
3. A *complicating action*—offering the sequences of events in the story.
4. An *evaluation*—suggesting the importance and meaning of the events in the story.
5. A *resolution*—informing us how the story ended.
6. A *coda*—returning the recitation of the story to the present time.

These six items are necessary for us to tell our stories to others and take care of the questions that might occur to our listeners as we progress. As she points out, when we converse and tell our stories, we must always keep in mind the question in the minds of our listeners: "and what comes next?"

Not all conversations involve stories; in some conversations, people discuss philosophical issues or politics, but in most personal conversations, sooner or later, people start telling stories about their experiences, about what happened to them in the past. And generally speaking, if Riessman is correct (that is, if Labov, whom she quotes, is correct) you find these six elements in the stories we tell in our conversations. That's because these rules are needed to give our listeners a means of following our stories. So if you happen to overhear parts of conversations when you are in airport terminals or restaurants or other places where large numbers of people are together, and you hear "and he said . . . and then she said . . . and then I said . . ." you should realize that you are hearing bits and pieces of the complicating action of the conversation. Conversations, then, are much more complex than we imagine. A French scholar of postmodernism, Jean-François Lyotard, suggested that when we speak we are, in certain ways, playing games—which means our conversations have rules and other factors connected with game playing. Bakhtin claimed that conversation involves thinking about what has been said and what will be said and that the dialogic aspects of conversation are of primary importance in communication. And an American scholar, Harold Garfinkel, did an experiment in which a member of a family adopted a formal style of conversation in a family setting. This drove other family members wild. And from Riessman and Laboy we get a list of the formal attributes of "fully formed" conversation.

In an article, "Narrative and Sociology," Laurel Richardson writes,

> Narrative is the primary way through which humans organize their experiences into temporally meaningful episodes. . . . Narrative is both a mode of reasoning *and* a mode of representation. People can "apprehend" the world narratively and people can "tell" about the world narratively. According to Jerome Bruner . . . narrative reasoning is one of the two basic and universal human cognition modes. The other mode is the logico-scientific. . . . The logico-scientific mode looks for universal truth conditions, whereas the narrative mode looks for particular connections between events. Explanation in the narrative mode is contextually embedded, whereas the logico-scientific explanation is extracted from spatial and temporal events. Both modes are "rational" ways of making meaning. (1990, 118)

So narratives play an important part in our lives, and the narratives we hear are one of the most important ways we make sense of the world. This power that narratives have applies, by extension, to what we learn from narratives that others create for us—in songs, in videos, in novels, in television shows, and in films.

n and Women Use Language Differently

ıry focus of my linguistic research always has been the language
■ of everyday conversation. One facet of this is conversational style: how different regional, ethnic, and class backgrounds, as well as age and gender, result in different ways of using language to communicate. *You Just Don't Understand* is about the conversational styles of women and men. As I gained more insight into typically male and female ways of using language, I began to suspect some of the causes of the troubling facts that women who go to single-sex schools do better in later life, and that when young women sit next to young men in classrooms, the males talk more. This is not to say that all men talk in class, nor that no women do. It is simply that a greater percentage of discussion time is taken by men's voices.

The research of sociologists and anthropologists ... has shown that girls and boys learn to use language differently in their sex-separate peer groups. Typically, a girl has a best friend with whom she sits and talks, frequently telling secrets. It's the telling of secrets, the fact and the way that they talk to each other, that makes them best friends. For boys, activities are central: Their best friends are the ones they do things with. Boys also tend to play in larger groups that are hierarchical. High-status boys give orders and push low-status boys around. So boys are expected to use language to seize center stage: by exhibiting their skill, displaying their knowledge, and challenging and resisting challenges.

— Deborah Tannen, "Teacher's Classroom Strategies Should Recognize That Men and Women Use Language Differently," *The Chronicle of Higher Education,* June 19, 1991

Questions for Discussion and Further Research

1. Have the media changed the conversational styles of men and women? Justify your answer.
2. What did Tannen find when she studied the conversational styles of boys and girls?
3. Charles Winick, a sociologist, has suggested that there is "desexualization" going on in America—that men are getting weaker and women stronger. Do you think he's right? If so, why might this be the case?
4. What implications does Tannen's research have for education in general, and teaching in particular?

The question that motivated Deborah Tannen's research on communication and gender involved trying to figure out why women who attended all-women's colleges did better in later life than women who attended coed institutions. What she discovered is that there is a difference between the way men and women use language in their sex-separate peer groups.

Girls, she discovered, tend to tell personal secrets to their best friends, while for boys, activities and rivalries are basic, and they gain a great deal of practice in using language to display their knowledge, fight off challenges, and challenge others. Because our classrooms tend to use, as Walter Ong explains, "ritual opposition," in which members of a class compete with one another for attention, girls are disadvantaged and boys are given a considerable advantage. Boys are raised in "adversativeness" and are thus, as a rule, much more assertive then girls.

In his book *The New People: Desexualization in American Life*, sociologist Charles Winick argues that sexual identity in America is being blurred and that women are becoming more masculine and men more feminine. He takes dancing as an example and writes,

> Havelock Ellis' beautiful metaphor of "the dance of life" reminds us that the dance once symbolized man-woman interaction, leading to the core of life and human society itself. But our new dances are openly anti-life, and symbolize a massive dislocation of sex roles. Rather than allowing

Men and Women Use Language Differently

for any definite leader and follower, as in the traditional courtship type of dance, the new style calls for autistic, self-absorbed actors. The essentially protective, defensive attitude of the urban man and woman taking care of himself or herself in a hard-edged, independent way is built right into the dance. (1968, 18)

He takes his theme of desexualization and shows how it can be seen in the names we give children, in the kinds of pets we have, in the kinds of heroes we find in the mass media, in our unisex fashions, and in many other areas. Winick published his book in 1968, but in an introduction to a new printing of his book in 1995, he sticks to his guns and argues that the phenomenon of desexualization that attracted his attention in the sixties hasn't changed significantly.

In my own experience, I found that my male students often were willing to respond to questions even if they didn't know the answer. That was because males have been trained, so to speak, to seize the spotlight. As a result of her research, Tannen concluded that in addition to the traditional lecture or seminar format for teaching, breaking classes up into small groups for collaborative learning exercises and activities, in which women were more comfortable, made very good sense. You will find a number of learning exercises at the end of this book that are designed to deal with the problem of male over-assertiveness.

Black Speech

We use folklore, then, as a familiar weapon for fighting a new battle. Songs, rhymes, and taunts change subject matter, but they retain the forms and formulas of childhood expression. To return to these devices is, in a large sense, regressive.

The Camingerly Negro not only goes through this regressive process when he reaches adolescence, but because of the necessity of remaining in a male world, he must continue to fight for a sense of control with essentially the same devices he learned in adolescence. This is amply illustrated by the large part rhyming plays in the life of the man of words. He not only uses traditional rhymes as part of his entertainment repertoire, but uses his abilities to insert rhymes that may entertain into any social situation. Such devices as "See you later, alligator" and "After 'while, crocodile" (which I am certain are Negro in origin) are found in much of the public discourse of these men. One day, for instance, while Kid and others were sitting around telling jokes, he said:

We can sit here and shuck and shive.
We can sit here and do the split.
We can sit here and do this.
We can sit here and shit.

Almost any cliché is stated in rhyme form. Here is a common dialogue routine illustrating this:

What you mean, jelly bean?
What I said, cabbage head....

Verbal combat accounts for a large portion of the talk between members of this group. Proverbs, turns of phrase, jokes, almost any manner of discourse is used not for purposes of discursive communication but as weapons in verbal battle. Any gathering of the men customarily turns into "sounding," a teasing or boasting session.

— Roger Abrahams, *Deep Down in the Jungle: Negro Narrative Folklore from the Streets of Philadelphia* (Chicago: Aldine, 1970), 43–45

(Note: The term "Negro" was commonly used for African Americans in the seventies when Abrahams wrote this book. Cameringly is a section in South Philadelphia where Abrahams did his research. Kid is the name of one of Abrahams's respondents.)

Questions for Discussion and Further Research

1. In what ways does Abrahams's essay agree with Tannen's?
2. How do black people from Camingerly use rhymes for entertainment and in social situations?
3. What does it mean to say that this rhyming behavior is "regressive"?
4. How might this rhyming behavior be manifested or utilized now in the mass media?
5. Can you find any other examples of verbal dueling in American society?

In 1963, Roger Abrahams, a folklorist, studied the patterns found in African American speech in an area of Philadelphia and found that this speech relied, to a considerable extent, on certain kinds of material that were familiar to the speakers from their childhood days. That is why he describes this use of forms and styles from the childhood of the speakers he studied as "regressive." The term *regression*, in psychoanalytic parlance, refers to momentarily returning to our childhood days, which is perfectly normal. When adults eat ice cream cones this is considered a momentary regression in the service of their egos—as they return to their childhood days when eating an ice cream cone was such a source of pleasure. From a Bakhtinian perspective, we would describe this use of the "forms and formulas" of childhood expression as intertextual—using sources we are familiar with in creating new texts.

Abrahams found that verbal dexterity, and, in particular, a talent for creating rhymes, played an important role in the verbal dueling that commonly occurred between adolescent African American males. These young men developed a remarkable talent not only for creating rhymes but also for inserting them everywhere—in all social situations.

It is possible to see a connection between this verbal dueling, based upon rhymes, and the development of rap music—in which this ability to create rhymes is given a beat and set to music. And the rhymed lyrics of many of these rap songs reflect a movement from personal dueling to social protest—though a number of rap artists, from many different ethnic and racial groups, have been condemned for sexist and other antisocial lyrics.

17 People of Color and the Media

Within current debates about race and difference, mass culture is the contemporary location that both publicly declares and perpetuates the idea that there is pleasure to be found in the acknowledgment and enjoyment of racial difference. The commodification of Otherness has been so successful because it is offered as a new delight, more intense, more satisfying than normal ways of doing and feeling. Within commodity culture, ethnicity becomes spice, seasoning that can liven up the dull dish that is mainstream white culture. Cultural taboos around sexuality and desire are transgressed and made explicit as the media bombards folk with a message of difference no longer based on the white supremacist assumption that "blondes have more fun." The "real fun" is to be had by bringing to the surface all those "nasty" unconscious fantasies and longings about contact with the Other embedded in the secret (not so secret) deep structure of white supremacy. In many ways it is a contemporary revival of interest in the "primitive," with a distinctly postmodern slant. As Marianna Torgovnick argues in *Gone Primitive: Savage Intellects, Modern Lives:*

> What is clear now is that the West's fascination with the primitive has to do with its own crises in identity, with its own need to clearly demarcate subject and object even while flirting with other ways of experiencing the universe.

Certainly from the standpoint of white supremacist capitalist patriarchy, the hope is that desires for the "primitive" or fantasies about the Other can be continually exploited, and that such exploitation will occur in a manner that reinscribes and maintains *the status quo.* Whether or not desire for contact with the Other . . . can act as a critical intervention challenging and subverting racial domination, inviting and enabling critical resistance is an unrealized political possibility.

— bell hooks, *Black Looks: Race and Representation* (Boston: South End Press, 1992), 179

Questions for Discussion and Further Research

1. Why does bell hooks assert that blondes don't have more fun anymore? Do you agree? Explain.
2. What does she mean by "otherness"? What role does it play in contemporary society?
3. What does she mean by "commodifying otherness"?
4. She asserts that ethnicity is now a "spice." What does she mean by that?
5. Define the terms in "white suprematist capitalist patriarchy." Do you agree with her on this subject?
6. How does she see the future of race relations in the United States? What role will the media play here?

This selection by bell hooks (she doesn't use capitals in her name) focuses on the matter of race and representation, the subject of much of her writings. In this passage, she calls attention to the fact that the media have moved beyond "blondes have more fun," and now present audiences with many different examples of "otherness," by which she means people of different colors, different races, and different ethnicities. What interests hooks is the unconscious desires that she alleges white people keep repressed as they fantasize about those who are different from themselves.

She also calls our attention to the fact that our fascination with so-called primitive people and people of color is connected, in subtle ways, to our own need to find our identities. Saussure suggested that concepts have meaning only in terms of their differences. It is relationships that help determine meaning and also identity. So our fascination with "otherness" is tied to our need to find out who we are. We are, from a Saussurean perspective, the opposite of those exhibiting "otherness," so by encountering them, we find out more about ourselves.

Our interest in those of different races and ethnicities, of those exhibiting "otherness," has been exploited by the media to help maintain the *status quo*. But hooks suggests that our fascination and desire for encounters with those exhibiting "otherness" may help challenge and subvert racial domination and thus may have revolutionary potentialities.

People of Color and the Media

18 ▸ Nonverbal Communication

Our speech-oriented culture is just beginning to take note of the profound and overlooked contribution of nonverbal behavior to the processes of communication. This contribution of our actions rather than our speech is especially important, since it is inseparable from the feelings that we knowingly or inadvertently project in our everyday social interaction and determines the effectiveness and well-being of our intimate, social, and working relationships. Indeed, in the realm of feelings, our facial expressions, postures, movements, and gestures are so important that when our words contradict the silent messages contained within them, others mistrust what we say—they rely almost completely on what we do. . . .

The present approach to the description of silent messages is one answer to "How is it possible to have consensus within and sometimes between cultures in using and understanding nonverbal signals when, unlike language, such matters are hardly ever explicitly discussed or taught?" The answer to this dilemma was that only a very few basic dimensions of human feelings and attitudes are conveyed nonverbally. These are variations in like-dislike, potency or status, and responsiveness. Each of these qualities is in turn related to a basic metaphor that provides the necessary link between the feeling, such as liking, and the behaviors which can reflect that feeling such as approaching. The shared metaphors (for example, people approach things they like and avoid things they dislike) make it possible to attain consensus in interpreting feelings along each of these dimensions. In addition, various combinations of these three dimensions allow us to express even the most subtle nuances of feeling.

The first of the three primary feeling dimensions requires little definition. The second, dominance, refers to a controlling versus a submissive and dependent attitude. Extreme examples are the dignified postures and movements of a monarch or those of a snob who exudes aloofness; these are in contrast with the shrinking posture of a weak and submissive person, which almost connotes "Don't hit me, please!"

Responsiveness refers to the extent of awareness of and the reaction to another. Alternatively, it reflects how much someone else, whether for good or bad reasons, is important or in the foreground for us.

— Albert Mehrabian, *Silent Messages* (Belmont, CA: Wadsworth, 1971), iii, v

Questions for Discussion and Further Research

1. Define "nonverbal" communication. How does it differ from verbal communication?
2. What are the three dimensions of human behavior that are expressed nonverbally?
3. Can you think of other dimensions that might be expressed non-verbally?
4. Why do we trust body language and facial expressions more than verbal messages?
5. Why do we react in certain ways to visual stimuli?

There are three important primary feelings that we communicate non-verbally, Mehrabian suggests: liking (or disliking), dominance, and responsiveness. What complicates matters is that we often combine these three primary feelings in different ways, which means we can communicate a considerable number of things by phenomena such as our facial expressions, movements, gestures, and body language.

If you turn off the sound when you watch commercials, you see the degree to which many of the actors and actresses in these little texts use very powerful body language, gestures, eye contact, and facial expressions (some of which are universal) to convince us to buy some product or service. We tend not to notice the extreme use of nonverbal communication when we listen to the commercials, but when we turn off the sound, we can see things more clearly, since we aren't distracted by what they are saying. In addition, there are editing techniques—such as extreme close-ups—that further intensify the power of this nonverbal communication.

Psychologists tell us we try to avoid communication that attacks or challenges our basic beliefs and values (cognitive dissonance) and look for reinforcement in communication that supports our beliefs and values. This might explain why the actors and actresses in commercials try so hard to be likable, to connect with us, to make us empathize with them. If we like them, then we can transfer these feelings of affection to the product or service they are advertising.

In his book *Visual Persuasion: The Role of Images in Advertising*, Paul Messaris offers an interesting insight. He writes,

Real-world vision is intimately connected with emotion, which, in turn, is tied to our functioning needs as biological and social creatures. When we look at the world, we are strongly predisposed to attend to certain kinds of objects or situations and to react in certain kinds of ways. These predispositions reflect the influence of culture, but . . . they have also been shaped to a certain extent by biological evolution. In short, real-world vision comes with a set of built-in response tendencies. (1997, 4)

One of the most important of these built-in tendencies is to look back at whoever is looking at us. Thus, in commercials, actors and actresses who look directly at us can count on a biologically coded response from us to look back at them.

A great deal of communication, we now recognize, is shaped by nonverbal factors. How you look and act when you address someone plays an important role in shaping the way the addressee will interpret and respond to what you say.

19 ► Facial Expressions

Faces are accessible "windows" into the mechanisms which govern our emotional and social lives. The technological means are now in hand to develop automated systems for monitoring facial expressions and animating artificial models. Face technology of the sort we describe, which is now feasible and achievable within a relatively short time frame, could revolutionize fields as diverse as medicine, law, communications, and education.

Facial expressions provide information about

- affective state, including both emotions such as fear, anger, enjoyment, surprise, sadness, disgust, and more enduring moods such as euphoria, dysphoria, or irritableness;
- cognitive activity, such as perplexity, concentration, or boredom;
- temperament and personality, including such traits as hostility, sociability, or shyness;
- truthfulness, including the leakage of concealed emotions and clues as to when the information provided in words about plans or actions is false;
- psychopathology, including not only diagnostic information relevant to depression, mania, schizophrenia, and other less severe disorders, but also information relevant to monitoring response to treatment.

In basic research on the brain, facial expressions can identify when specific mental processes are occurring, periods that can be examined with new imaging technologies. . . . Facial expressions also hold promise for applied medical research, for example, in identifying the role of emotions and moods in coronary artery disease.

In education, the teacher's facial expressions influence whether the pupils learn, and the pupil's facial expressions can inform the teacher of the need to adjust the instructional message.

In criminal justice contexts, facial expressions play a crucial role in establishing or detracting from credibility. In business, facial expressions are important in negotiations and personnel decisions. In medicine, facial expressions can be useful in studies of the autonomic nervous system and the psychological state of the patient.

— Paul Ekman and Terrence J. Sejnowski, *Facial Expression Understanding* (Executive Summary of report to the National Science Foundation), August 1, 1992, http://face-and-emotion.com/dataface/nsfrept/exec_summary.html (accessed July 14, 2005)

Questions for Discussion and Further Research

1. List and discuss the areas facial expressions give information about.
2. How do poker players deal with the problem of facial expression giving away information?
3. Research what has been found about which muscles express which emotions in the face.
4. Why do we feel emotions when we are watching performers pretend to feel things in texts?
5. Do you think any facial expressions are universal? If so, which ones? Justify your position.
6. Are facial expressions gender specific? If so, which ones? Explain your answer.
7. If we can automate reading facial expressions, do you think that will be good or bad?

Over the past forty years, psychologist Paul Ekman and other social scientists have been exploring facial expressions and what they reveal about our emotional states and other matters. In the passage above, which comes from a report to the National Science Foundation, Ekman and Sejnowski point out how useful studying facial expression is for any number of different areas.

Our facial expressions, the authors point out, reveal many things about us, which they list. They show these things for those who know how to read faces. (We read faces when we read people, but most of us are amateurs and don't really know how to do either.) What is interesting about this report is that it suggests that it is now possible to automate reading facial expressions, which could have important implications for many different areas. For example, lawyers now hire so-called experts to help them select juror members who will be friendly to their point of view. These experts use the information that Ekman and others provide in books and articles. This expertise in reading faces for emotions can also be used in medicine, and, as the authors point out, in some cases facial expressions can indicate emotions that may be connected to coronary artery disease.

Reading faces is, as I see things, a branch of applied semiotics, and Ekman has appeared at semiotic conferences to explain his research. When we read a face we look for certain signs that express or indicate emotions, moods, and other phenomena. What semiotics tells us is that we are always sending messages—with our facial expressions, body language, clothes, use of language, and so on—and others are reading those messages, at the same time that they are sending us messages about themselves.

haracteristics at birth are the basis for the "script" identifying social expectations for sex-appropriate behavior. Recent research has shown that very early in life, before children are aware of sexual differences, they are alerted to differences in dress, and that as early as two years of age they classify people according to gender. Gender scripts help to create two social categories, the members of which deal with their bodies differently. . . . Men are socialized to use their bodies in a straightforward manner: they learn to manipulate, grasp, and hold. Women learn to convey the feeling that their bodies are delicate and precious: they are supposed to caress objects and people.

Psychologist J.C. Flugel suggested that the basis for sex-specific attire is sexual *interdependence.* He noted that visual distinction between the sexes has been seen throughout history. . . . Everyone assumes that people wear sex-specific attire because doing so follows "The natural order of things." Sex-specific attire was, and is, intended to alert an approaching individual about *suitability for sexual intercourse.* Even articles of clothing associated with a specific sex have the power to arouse passion in members of the other sex. The tie, jacket, trousers, and shoes of the male, for example, and the high heels, garter, and girdle associated with the female have been found to elicit sexual responses. Hence, the purpose of sex-specific attire is to spur interaction between the two sexes. Survival of the species depends on such a distinction.

British costume historian James Laver suggested that sex-specific attire identifies the social spheres in which men and women function. The "hierarchy principle" underlies male dress. Men wear class-conscious attire that reflects their standing in the wider social sphere. Female attire is governed by the seductive principle. It is designed to make women attractive to men and hence less significant.

— Ruth P. Rubinstein, *Dress Codes: Meanings and Messages in American Culture* (Boulder, CO: Westview, 1995), 83

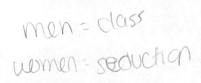

men = class

women = seduction

Questions for Discussion and Further Research

1. What does the author say about the differences between the ways men and women use their bodies?
2. What is a gender script? How do these gender scripts function?
3. What did Flugel say about clothes and sexuality? Do you agree? Justify your answer.
4. What did Laver say about the social spheres of men and women and dress? Do you agree? Explain.
5. How is fashion "collective behavior"?
6. What is the irony of fashion?

Fashion, we must realize, is a form of collective behavior, and as such it is of interest to social scientists trying to understand why people behave the way they do. There are some cultures where people have been wearing the same costumes for hundreds of years. Generally there is a correlation between lack of change in fashion and socioeconomic backwardness. In most countries there is a considerable interest in fashion, and people constantly keep changing their styles. Rubinstein is interested in the "gender scripts" that fashions entail—in how men's fashions lead to a sense of how they should use their bodies and how women's fashions suggest that their bodies are "precious" and that their gender should be a nurturing one, one that caresses objects and people. She discusses the ideas of several other scholars, who have interesting insights to offer about fashion.

Rubinstein mentions the work of a psychologist, J. C. Flugel, who argues that fashion is tied to people's sexuality. Women's fashion is based, he argues, on showing their "suitability for sexual intercourse." This feeling is created not only by the clothes women wear but also by other articles that enhance the sexual message of their clothes. Men's clothes—ties, jackets, trousers, and shoes—elicit sexual excitement in women, Flugel argues. Fashion, then, plays a major role in making sure that men and women become excited by one another, which is necessary for the survival of the species. If you look at magazines such as *Vanity Fair* and *Glamour*, you see page after page of glamorous models, seductively dressed, semianorexic, looking as if they have just had sex or are anticipating it any moment. The lighting of the photographs and the editing contribute to this seductiveness and to their becoming "sex objects."

Another scholar Rubinstein mentions is costume historian James Laver, who focuses his attention on the social spheres in which men and women move. He argues that in men's clothing, there is a "hierarchy principle" that shows where the men belong in the class system. Women's fashion, on the other hand, is based on a "seductive principle" and is designed to make women desirable to men—and thus gives them a secondary status in the scheme of things. That is, if women's main function is to be desirable sex objects for men, they are less important than men.

Fashion is also connected with our consumer culture, for to be fashionable, we must do a good deal of shopping, to purchase items that have become "hot" or fashionable. Fashion can be construed more broadly than garments. Certain objects become fashionable—iPods, for example—and there is a mad rush to obtain them. After a while, they lose their power as our attention becomes distracted by something else—a new fashionable place to vacation, a fashionable beauty treatment, and so forth. Levis used to be fashionable. Then, suddenly, teenagers abandoned them for other brands, such as Diesel. Levis has spent a great deal of money trying to figure out what happened and how they can lure teenagers and others back—so far, without much success.

There is also an irony to fashion. People who are shy and don't wish to call attention to themselves are forced to follow the fashion; otherwise they would attract attention because they look different from everyone else. Teenagers, who spend a good deal of money on being fashionable, are notoriously fickle, so it is difficult to be able to determine how to design and market for them. Fashion must be understood to be a very powerful force for most people. There are some who do not care about fashions and dress and live according to their own dictates, but they are a relatively small proportion of the populace.

21 Symbolism and Religion

The Middle Ages never forgot that all things would be absurd, if their meaning were exhausted in their function and their place in the phenomenal world, if by their essence they did not reach into a world beyond this. This idea of a deeper significance in ordinary things is familiar to us as well, independently of religious convictions: as an indefinite feeling which may be called up at any moment, by the sound of raindrops on the leaves or by the lamplight on the table. . . . "When we see all things in God, and refer all things to Him, we read in common matters superior expressions of meaning." [W. James: *Varieties of Religious Experience,* p. 474] .

Here, then, is the psychological foundation from which symbolism arises. In God nothing is empty of sense: *nihil vacuum neque sine signo apud Deum,* said Saint Irenaeus. So the conviction of a transcendental meaning in all things seeks to formulate itself. About the figure of the Divinity a majestic system of correlated figures crystallizes, which all have reference to Him, because all things derive their meaning from Him. The world unfolds itself like a vast whole of symbols, like a cathedral of ideas. It is the most richly rhythmical conception of the world, a polyphonous expression of eternal harmony. . . .

From the causal point of view, symbolism appears as a sort of short-circuit of thought. Instead of looking for the relation between two things by following the hidden detours of their causal connections, thought makes a leap and discovers their relation, not in a connection of cause or effects, but in a connection of signification or finality.

— Johan Huizinga, *The Waning of the Middle Ages* (Garden City, NY: Anchor Books, 1924), 201–203

Questions for Discussion and Further Research

1. What did Huizinga say about religious belief and the hidden significance of ordinary things?
2. In an age of science, what do people think about symbols and their role in our everyday lives?
3. What's the difference between manifest and latent functions?
4. Why don't people recognize the hidden meanings and unconscious significance of what they do?
5. Discuss the way religious and other symbols are used in a specific film, television show, advertisement, or commercial.

Johan Huizinga's study of the Middle Ages offers us an important insight into the mindset of people in this period of time—the fourteenth and fifteenth centuries, a period of powerful religious belief marked by extreme behavior: asceticism on one side and licentiousness on the other. In those days, people found meaning and significance in everything because, from their world view, everything was connected to God. If, in God, nothing is empty of sense, then everything is tied to God, and it is the duty of people to recognize this situation and thus find symbolic religious significance in everything. Seemingly common matters, as William James reminds us, have important meaning for the religious mind.

Although we now live in an age of science, this notion that symbols connect us to the divine is still believed by many people. And for those who aren't certain that God exists, or don't believe God exists, symbols are still important—as the selection from Jung in the next chapter and as the theories of Freud suggest—for they help connect us to unconscious parts of our psyches. It can be argued that the psychoanalytic perspective strips away the religious aspects of symbolism but uses symbols for its own purposes—to investigate the human psyche. This is because of the power of symbols. If you believe that a transcendental meaning can be found in all things, you will believe that seemingly simple objects can have very powerful emotional effects on people, which leads Huizinga to suggest that trivial and commonplace things often do a better job of revealing the character of an age than philosophy and other kinds of abstract speculation.

This notion—that there are hidden meanings in seemingly trivial things people do and say and in commonplace objects they use—is, in fact, a basic premise of the social sciences. It is precisely because people do not recognize the unconscious significance of their actions that we need psychologists and anthropologists and other kinds of social scientists. For example, sociologists distinguish between manifest and latent functions of behavior. The manifest function

Symbolism and Religion

is the reason we give when we are asked why we did something. The latent function, sociologists would argue, would be the unconscious reason we do something. Thus, the manifest function of working on a political campaign might be to help elect a certain candidate, while the latent function might be to meet a potential sexual partner. Nothing, then, is as simple as it might seem because so many things we do are loaded with symbolic significance.

The Meaning of Symbols

What we call a symbol is a term, a name, or even a picture that may be familiar in daily life, yet that possesses specific connotations in addition to its conventional and obvious meaning. It implies something vague, unknown, or hidden from us.... Thus a word or an image is symbolic when it implies something more than its obvious and immediate meaning. It has a wider "unconscious" aspect that is never precisely defined or fully explained. Nor can one hope to define or explain it. As the mind explores the symbol, it is led to ideas that lie beyond the grasp of reason....

Because there are innumerable things beyond the range of human understanding, we constantly use symbolic terms to represent concepts that we cannot define or fully comprehend. This is one reason why all religions employ symbolic language or images. But this conscious use of symbols is only one aspect of a psychological fact of great importance. Man also produces symbols unconsciously and spontaneously, in the form of dreams.

It is not easy to grasp this point. But the point must be grasped if we are to know more about the ways in which the human mind works. Man, as we realize if we reflect for a moment, never perceives anything fully or comprehends anything completely. He can see, hear, touch, and taste, but how far he sees, how well he hears, what his touch tells him and what he tastes depend upon the number and quality of his senses.... There are certain events of which we have not consciously taken note: they have remained, so to speak, below the threshold of consciousness. They have happened but they have been absorbed subliminally, without our conscious knowledge.

— Carl G. Jung, *Man and His Symbols* (New York: Laurel, 1968), 3–5

Questions for Discussion and Further Research

1. How does Jung define a symbol? How can words or images be symbolic?
2. Why does Jung say that "man never perceives anything fully or comprehends anything completely"?
3. Explain Peirce's trichotomy of icon, index, and symbol. Give your own examples of each.
4. Explain what Jung meant by archetypes and the collective unconscious.
5. What role has the "symbolic" played in your life? Be specific.

The term *symbol* comes from the Greek *symbolon* and means, literally, a token. We use the term symbol as something that stands for something else. Symbols are also used in psychoanalytic thought to stand for something generally repressed in the unconscious. The semiotician Charles Sanders Peirce had a trichotomy that is one of the central elements in his theory of signs. He argued that signs communicate three ways:

Kind of Sign	Method of Communication	Example	Process
1. Icon	Resemblance	Picture	Can see
2. Index	Causal connection	Smoke/fire	Figure out
3. Symbol	Convention	Flag	Learn

Symbols, then, don't have any meaning in themselves; we have to give symbols meaning and teach others what various symbols mean. And their meaning is shaped by historical events and other kinds of things. Words are symbols; so are flags and certain objects that have a historical or religious significance (think of the cross, the crescent, the Star of David).

Jung makes an important point when he suggests that the process by which we learn the meaning of certain symbols is unconscious—that we absorb them in a subliminal manner. He also suggests that symbols have a power to suggest hidden realms that we cannot fathom in a conscious manner. That is why works of art that rely on symbols have such power, and the same applies to religions, which make great use of symbolism. Jung had a theory that there are what he called "archetypes," such as the hero and the myth of paradise, that are part of a so-called collective unconscious of all people and are universal. This theory has been the subject of considerable controversy. But there is no question that symbols play an important role in the communication process and have the power to speak to people in ways we still do not completely understand.

23 ► The House as a Symbol of Femininity

As the car is the symbol of masculinity, so is the house a symbol of femininity. To a woman, her home is like another, larger body and all her mysterious impulses find expression within its walls. Her deepest self is implicated in the texture of the draperies, the casual shape of chairs and tables, the dimensions of a bed. As she trudges from shop to shop—examining, comparing, pondering over this article or that—her choices are determined by an unconscious image of what she is, or dreads to be. . . .

The unconscious fear of "exposing" not their taste alone but their inmost selves is what drives a large number of women into the arms of professional decorators. By leaving decisions to the experts, they disengage themselves from the entire project. Or try to. . . .

For instance . . . a girl with a strong unconscious masculine identification may adopt a starkly modernistic decor; its clean straight lines and lack of protuberances announce plainly the kind of body she would like to have had. But, if she is struggling against this tendency, she may feel the compulsion to "say it isn't so" and fill her home, as an acquaintance of mine did, with plump chairs and sofas in the Biedermaier style. This woman, incidentally, solved her conflict rather neatly. Her own study—where she pursued her scholarly researches and to which she rarely admitted anybody else—was in marked contrast to the rest of her house, severely functional, with not a curve in sight. It did not resemble her body, which was as stout and cushiony as the publicly displayed furniture. But it did give visible form to the unconscious idea she had of herself, an idea further manifested in her lean and sinewy prose.

— Milton R. Sapirstein, MD, *Paradoxes of Everyday Life* (New York: Premier Books, 1955), 95–98

Questions for Discussion and Further Research

1. Why is a car a symbol of masculinity?
2. How did Sapirstein explain that a house is a symbol of femininity?
3. Do you think the example he used makes sense? Justify your opinion.
4. How did Brenner explain "reaction formation"?
5. Does "reaction formation" mean that symbols can mean anything we want them to? Justify your answer.
6. Investigate "condensation" and "displacement" and explain how they function in dreams.

Milton Sapirstein is a psychoanalyst who analyzes various paradoxical aspects of human behavior. He focuses in this selection on the symbolic significance of houses. The way that houses are decorated, he suggests, exposes hidden and unconscious aspects of many women's psyches. He focuses on women here because in American culture it is generally women who make the decisions about how a house is to be furnished. This, fortunately, has been changing to some degree in recent years.

Thus, he argues, a woman with an unconscious masculine identification may very well adopt a certain decorating style—in this case modernistic with straight lines and a lack of protuberances (symbolically representing breasts) that expresses the kind of body she would like to have had. On the other hand, a woman with this unconscious masculine identification may go in the other direction and fill a house full of plump chairs and sofas. This would be an expression of what psychoanalysts describe as reaction formation.

Charles Brenner, a psychiatrist, describes reaction formation in his book *An Elementary Textbook of Psychoanalysis* in the following manner:

House as Symbol

> This is a mechanism whereby one of a pair of ambivalent attitudes, e.g., hate, is rendered unconscious and kept unconscious by an overemphasis on the other, which in this example would be love. Thus hate *appears* to be replaced by love, cruelty by gentleness, stubbornness by compliance, pleasure in dirt by neatness and cleanliness, and so on, yet the missing attitude persists unconsciously. (1973, 84)

The House as a Symbol of Femininity

This means that our behavior can, at times, be difficult to fathom, for a certain behavior can be an authentic expression of love but it also can be an expression of hate that has been suppressed and expressed as love due to a reaction formation.

Since symbols play an important role in our lives, the existence of this phenomenon of reaction formation makes it difficult to determine what anything means. A billowy sofa and soft chairs can be an expression of femininity or its reverse, an unconscious masculine sense of one's body. In addition, our dreams are full of symbols whose meaning is often hard to fathom, since we disguise our intentions by condensation and displacement. Saussure's and Freud's ideas about the role of oppositions in language and in our thinking are relevant here. Because of the nature of language, we find ourselves thinking, feeling, and acting in terms of the polar oppositions that help give meaning to life.

24 Miss America's Mythic Significance

Is it merely illusory or anachronistic to discern in the multiplying pageants of the Miss America, Miss Universe, Miss College Queen type a resurgence of the cults of the pre-Christian fertility goddesses? Perhaps it is. But students of the history of religions have become less prone in recent years to dismiss out of hand the possibility that the cultural behavior of modern man may be significantly illuminated by studying it in the perspective of the mythologies of bygone ages. After all, did not Freud initiate a revolution in social science by utilizing the venerable myth of Oedipus to help make sense out of the strange behavior of his Viennese contemporaries? Mircea Eliade has reminded us that although twentieth-century man may be consciously "post-Christian," his unconscious still seethes with religious symbols that display interesting similarities to those of archaic religions.

In light of this fertile combination of insights from modern social science and history of religions, it is no longer possible to see in the Miss America Pageant merely an over-publicized prank foisted on us by the advertising industry. It certainly is this, but it is also much more. It represents the mass cultic celebration, complete with a rich variety of ancient ritual embellishments, of the growing place of The Girl in the collective soul of America.

This young woman—though she is no doubt totally ignorant of the fact—symbolizes something beyond herself. She symbolizes The Girl, the primal image, the One behind the Many. . . . The Girl is also the omnipresent ikon of consumer society. Selling beer she is folksy and jolly. Selling gems she is chic and distant. . . . In Miss America's glowingly healthy smile, her openly sexual but officially virginal figure, and in the name-brand gadgets around her, she personifies the stunted aspirations and ambivalent fears of her culture.

— Harvey Cox, "Miss America and the Cult of the Girl," *Christianity and Crisis* (August 7, 1961)

Questions for Discussion and Further Research

1. Why does Cox argue that Miss America is a mythic figure?
2. What points does Cox make about how Miss America functions in American society? He wrote this article before the development of feminist thought. Has that led to significant changes in the role of "the girl" in American culture?
3. Investigate Freud's theory of the Oedipus complex and explain how he believed it functions.
4. Discuss some "mythic motifs" found in a specific film, television show, video, song, or other media text.
5. Ratings suggest that there is less interest now in traditional beauty contests like Miss America. Why do you think this has happened? Could it be connected to Charles Winick's thesis about desexualization in America?

In his essay on Miss America and the numerous other contests of a similar nature (such as Miss Universe), Cox deals with a number of topics that have been dealt with in this book. One thing he does is deal with the symbolic significance of Miss America figures. This takes up a thread of thought developed by Freud and Jung about the significance of symbols. Symbolic heroes, as Jung points out, play an important role in our lives, connecting to unconscious elements in our psyches. Then, taking a cue from Mircea Eliade, a scholar of religious thought, Cox ties these contests to ancient myths and rites, pointing out that our behavior can be understood more fully by recognizing the degree to which modern practices are tied to ancient myths. As Eliade has written in *The Sacred and the Profane: The Nature of Religion,*

> A whole volume could be written on the myths of modern man, on the mythologies camouflaged in the plays that he enjoys, the books that he reads. The cinema, that "dream factory," takes over and employs countless mythical motifs—the fight between hero and monster, initiatory combats and ordeals, paradigmatic figures and images (the maiden, the hero, the paradisal landscape, hell, and so on). (1961, 205)

Paradigmatic figures can be defined as ones that are typical and exemplary—more or less models for others to follow. Miss America, as Cox suggests, can be seen as connected to a resurgence, in modified form, of a long line of fertility goddesses from ancient days.

She also represents, Cox argues, a celebration of "the girl" in American culture. And her job, like so many other figures, is to function as an icon of

American consumer culture—that is where her real significance lies and is her most important function. In this respect, Cox's ideas are relevant to the chapters that follow, with selections by Cortese and Haug, which deal with advertising's impact on the behavior of women—not only in America but in Germany and elsewhere. In recent years, as the media have coarsened American culture (as well as other cultures where mass-mediated pop culture is all-pervasive), the virginal Miss America figure has been replaced by female icons like Madonna and Britney Spears and others who exude sexual desire in their videos, which, in many cases, can be described as semipornographic. Miss America and the other similar beauty pageants reflect an innocence that has been lost, replaced by women who have abandoned the "virginal" and innocent quality of these beauty queens and who now exploit their bodies and their sexuality to sell their songs and videos.

In this respect I recall reading an article recently in a newspaper in which a prostitute was bemoaning the fact that so many high school students and college students now look and dress like prostitutes that real prostitutes find it hard to figure out a way to dress to attract potential customers. We have come a long way from the days when clean-cut Miss America figures functioned as culture heroines and millions of young girls could dream about having someone sing to them, "There she is, Miss America."

Cox wrote this article before the development of feminist thought and changes in our notions of the role of women in society, so his analysis of the mythic significance of the beauty pageant may be somewhat dated. On the other hand, his analysis of the role that more modern or "hip" evocations of "the girl"—beautiful models, fashionable celebrities, "hot" women athletes, and glamorous movie stars—play in contemporary consumer culture still seems to be on the mark.

25 Images of Women in Advertising

Advertisers have an enormous financial stake in a narrow ideal of femininity that they promote, especially in beauty product ads.... The image of the ideal beautiful woman ... may perhaps be captured with the concept of the *provocateur* (an ideal image that arouses a feeling or reaction). The exemplary female prototype in advertising, regardless of product or service, displays youth (no lines or wrinkles), good looks, sexual seductiveness ... and perfection (no scars, blemishes, or even pores).

The provocateur is not human; rather, she is a form or hollow shell representing a female figure. Accepted attractiveness is her only attribute. She is slender, typically tall and long-legged.... Women are constantly held to this unrealistic standard of beauty. If they fail to attain it, they are led to feel guilty and ashamed. Cultural ideology tells women that they will not be desirable to, or loved by, men unless they are physically perfect....

This ultimate image is not real. It can only be achieved artificially through the purchase of vast quantities of beauty products.... The perfect provocateur is a mere façade. Even the models themselves do not look in the flesh as impeccable as they are depicted in ads. The classic image is constructed through cosmetics, photography, and airbrushing techniques.

Although the feminist movement challenged this "beauty myth," ... the beauty industries (i.e. cosmetics, fashion, diet, and cosmetic surgery) countered with a multidimensional attack. First, they simply increased the number of commercial beauty images to which women are exposed. More than $1 million is spent every hour on cosmetics. Most of that money is spent on advertising and packaging. Only eight cents of the cosmetics sale dollar goes to pay for ingredients; the rest goes to packaging, promotion, and marketing.

— Anthony J. Cortese, *Provocateur: Images of Women and Minorities in Advertising,* 2nd ed. (Lanham, MD: Rowman & Littlefield, 2004), 53–54

Questions for Discussion and Further Research

1. How does Cortese define the "provocateur"?
2. What role does she play in advertising in America, according to Cortese?
3. Do you agree with Cortese or disagree with him? Justify your position with detailed arguments.
4. Why do you think the "beauty myth" has been resistant to feminist attacks?
5. Defend or attack this statement: "The cosmetic industry is based on a faith in magic."

Anthony J. Cortese offers a powerful critique of the way that the advertising industry has "packaged" women and offered, as ideals, what most accurately can be described as unreal, rather freakish, long-legged, size four anorexic models. The term he uses for these models is *provocateurs*, and what they are supposed to provoke are sexual fantasies in the minds of women who identity with these models and, for most women, terrible anxieties because they cannot measure up to the physical "perfection" of their ideals. Ordinary women become anxious because they fear that men desire only these ideals of perfection because that is what our cultural ideology demands. So women who are not young, who do not have the requisite figure, whose hair isn't as glossy and full of life as it might be, and whose skin might not be as smooth as a baby's are supposed to (and often do) become terribly afraid.

This cultural ideology is created by the advertising industry, which plays upon the anxieties women have about their beauty and desirability in various beauty product print advertisements and television commercials. We have seen that clothes styles are used by the fashion industry to produce what feminists describe as "sex objects," women whose fashion statements are meant to be sexually exciting to others—generally to men, but not always so. And subordinate, as well.

Cortese points out that photographs can be air brushed to eliminate imperfections and that the glamour of these models is connected to the way photographers can manipulate images. In real life, the models aren't as "perfect" as they seem in advertisements. The final irony is that most of the money women (and now, increasingly men) spend on cosmetics goes for packaging and advertising. Only eight cents of every dollar is spent on the actual ingredients in cosmetics. Using cosmetics can be thought of as a behavior based on magical thinking that people do, assuming that a touch of this perfume or using that lipstick will do the job of turning them from a sexless hausfrau into a goddess of beauty. Once a woman starts thinking magically, she is open to new products that claim to do whatever she wants them to do. There is no way to use logic in such situations, because the magical thinker is convinced that any lack of success is due to using the wrong product, so the endless search goes on.

As we shall see in the next selection, by the German social scientist Wolfgang Haug, there are seemingly rational aspects to dressing fashionably—in the hunt for sexual partners—though Haug argues that they aren't as rational as they might seem to be. And that is because when sex walks into the room, rationality flies out the window.

The Power of Advertising in Capitalist Societies

A dvertising transfers its breadth of experience and calculation to its target groups. It treats its human targets like commodities, to whom it offers the solution to their problem of realization. Clothes are advertised like packaging as a means of sales promotion. This is one of the many ways in which commodity aesthetics takes possession of people.

The two central areas in which advertising offers, by means of commodities, to solve the problems of "scoring hits" and sales are, on the one hand, following a career of the labour market and, on the other, gaining the respect of and attracting others. "How is it that clever and competent people don't make it in their careers?" was the question put by a wool advertisement in 1968. "Don't call it bad luck if it is only a matter of 'packaging.' You can sell yourself better in a new suit! And that is often what counts in life." A woman whose romance has failed and who is looking for a new partner was recommended by *Twen* magazine in 1969, as "step 9" in its advice, to "become overwhelmingly pretty. . . . Why not try what you've never tried before? If you want to scour the market, you've got to show yourself in your best packaging." Where love succeeds, brought about by this fashionable packaging, and leads to encounters which under existing conditions appear in the form of a commodity-cash nexus, the cost of clothes can be interpreted as "capital investment."

— Wolfgang Haug, *Critique of Commodity Aesthetics: Appearance, Sexuality and Advertising in Capitalist Society* (Minneapolis: University of Minnesota Press, 1986), 72–73

Questions for Discussion and Further Research

1. What does Haug mean when he says advertising treats people like commodities?
2. How have stores made consumption a form of pleasure? Be specific.
3. What areas does Haug suggest advertising focuses upon?
4. Is it correct to suggest that clothes are little more than "packaging"? Explain your position.
5. Why does Haug argue that advertising leads to self-alienation?

As the title of his book suggests, Haug is interested in the aesthetic as well as the economic aspects of capitalist societies. He argues that the people who sell to us have used aesthetics in very effective ways to seduce us into becoming consumers. Consumption is no longer a task but has been turned into a source of pleasure in stores that recognize how to make themselves appealing and make the shopping experience a source of joy.

He takes the example of the way advertising claims to help us with two important areas of our lives—our jobs and our sexuality. You can sense the sarcasm he feels when he quotes a wool advertiser arguing that packaging plays an important role in the business world and telling its readers, "You can sell yourself better in a new suit." Then he quotes from a German magazine, *Twen*, that advised a woman with a failed romance to "become overwhelmingly pretty." This, it argues, is connected to the correct packaging. "If you want to scour the market, you've got to show yourself in your best packaging."

Thus human beings are reduced to objects, not too different, perhaps, from peanut butter, coffee, or laundry soap, that need to be packaged correctly to sell themselves. Clothes, from this point of view, can be seen as capital investments that can be expected to pay off—either in a better job or a new romance. Haug is articulating what probably goes on in the minds of many people who follow the dictates of fashions and who believe that "clothes make the man," who then, it is implied, will be able to find the woman of his heart's desire (and vice versa).

Advertising has been used, Haug argues, to make men and women develop new relationships with their bodies. In the cases dealt with above, there is a suggestion of estrangement and separation from one's body. It is merely one more commodity, something to be packaged to get the right job or the right sexual partners. The problem is that when we treat our bodies as commodities, we pay a very high price because we must, by necessity, become estranged and alienated from ourselves.

The Power of Advertising in Capitalist Societies

27 ▶ Myths and Society

This book has a double theoretical framework: on the one hand, an ideological critique bearing on the language of so-called mass-culture; on the other, a first attempt to analyze semiologically the mechanics of this language. I had just read Saussure and as a result acquired the conviction that by treating "collective representations" as sign-systems, one might hope to go further than the pious show of unmasking them and account *in detail* for the mystification which transforms petite-bourgeois culture into a universal nature. . . .

The following essays were written one each month for about two years, from 1954 to 1956, on topics suggested by current events. I was at the time trying to reflect regularly on some myths of French daily life. . . . The starting point of these reflections was usually a feeling of impatience at the sight of "naturalness" with which newspapers, art and common sense constantly dress up a reality which even though it is the one we live in, is undoubtedly determined by history. In short, in the account given of our contemporary circumstances, I resented seeing Nature and History confused at every turn, and I wanted to track down, in the decorative display of *what-goes-without-saying,* the ideological abuse which, in my view, is hidden there . . . .

I was already certain of a fact from which I tried to draw all the consequences: myth is a language. So that while concerning myself with phenomena apparently most unlike literature (a wresting match, an elaborate dish, a plastics exhibition), I did not feel I was leaving the field of this general semiology of our bourgeois world, the literary aspects of which I had begun to study in earlier essays.

— Roland Barthes, *Mythologies* (New York: Hill & Wang, 1972), 9, 11

Questions for Discussion and Further Research

1. What does it mean to treat "collective representations" as sign systems?
2. How does Barthes distinguish between the "natural" and the "historical"? Why is this important?
3. What is the definition of "ideology"? How might ideology be "hidden" in wrestling and plastics?
4. Why is "what-goes-without-saying" important for Barthes's critique of bourgeois capitalism?
5. If Roland Barthes were writing about America, what topics might he choose to analyze? Why?

Roland Barthes was one of the most influential literary and culture theorists of recent years, and *Mythologies* is probably his most well-known book. Barthes defines myth in a somewhat different manner than other scholars, emphasizing the hidden ideological content of such things as televised professional wrestling, soap powders, margarine, toys, the striptease, and plastic. What Barthes did, in each of his essays in the first part of his book, was to reveal the mystifications found in the way popular culture and everyday life is presented to the public—in this case, the French public. The second part of the book, "Myth Today," is theoretical and offers his speculations on the relation between semiology (this term has been replaced by *semiotics*) and cultural myths found in France. In this section he argues that "Myth is not defined by the object of its message, but by the way in which it utters this message (1972, 109). So it is the way objects, people, and events are characterized by the media that is of interest to him.

Mythologies is characterized by fascinating insights into aspects of everyday things that generally escape our attention. For example, in his analysis of soap powders and detergents he notices that the detergent Omo claims it cleans "deep," which implies, if you follow the logic of the situation, that linen is deep—since it is linens and other clothes that Omo is used to clean. Physically speaking, linen is thin, but psychologically speaking, if Omo is correct, linen sheets and other kinds of linen are "deep." He contrasts Omo with Persil, a soap power that separates or liberates linen from dirt, but mentions in the conclusion of his essay that they are similar in one very important respect—they are both owned by Unilever, an Anglo-Dutch trust.

Myth, Barthes suggests, is on the right, politically, which means it is the task of the semiologist/semiotician to uncover and expose the hidden ideological assumptions found in mass-mediated culture. Barthes wrote another book similar in nature to *Mythologies* about Japan, which he called *Empire of Signs*. In this book Barthes was not interested in ideology but in fascinating aspects of Japanese culture revealed in a number of important signifiers of that culture (what Barthes would call "Japaneseness") such as Japanese chopsticks, tempura, bowing, and Pachinko.

The important thing we learn from Barthes is to look at texts, rituals, objects, and other aspects of everyday life as signs, which means they have meanings that can be elicited from them, if one has an understanding of the principles of semiotics and of the way myths inform our activities, our media, and our cultures. The Canadian media theorist and analyst Marshall McLuhan had the same idea and analyzed comic strips, advertisements, and other similar phenomena in his book *The Mechanical Bride*. Barthes was familiar with McLuhan's work, and it is possible that he was influenced by *The Mechanical Bride*, which appeared a few years before Barthes started writing his *Mythologies*.

28 ▸ Robinson Crusoe as Myth

We do not usually think of *Robinson Crusoe* as a novel. Defoe's first full-length work of fiction seems to fall more naturally into place with *Faust, Don Juan,* and *Don Quixote,* the great myths of our civilization. What these myths are about it is fairly easy to say. Their basic plots, their enduring images, all exhibit a single-minded pursuit by the protagonist of one of the characteristic aspirations of Western man. . . . Don Quixote, the impetuous generosity and limiting blindness of chivalric idealism; Don Juan pursuing and at the same time tormented by the idea of boundless experience of women; Faustus, the great knower, whose curiosity, always unsatisfied, causes him to be damned. . . .

Crusoe lives in the imagination mainly as a triumph of human achievement and enterprise, and as a favorite example of the elementary processes of political economy. . . . *Robinson Crusoe* is related to three essential themes of modern civilization—which we can briefly designate as "Back to Nature," "The Dignity of Labor," and "Economic Man." *Robinson Crusoe* seems to have become a kind of culture hero representing all three of these related but not wholly congruent ideas. It is true that if we examine what Defoe actually wrote and what he may be thought to have intended, it appears that *Robinson Crusoe* hardly supports some of the symbolic uses to which the pressure of the needs of our society has made it serve. But this, of course, is in keeping with the status of *Robinson Crusoe* as a myth, for we learn as much from the varied shapes that a myth takes in men's minds as from the form in which it first arose. It is not an author but a society that metamorphoses a story into a myth, by retaining only what its unconscious needs dictate and forgetting everything else.

— Ian Watt, "Robinson Crusoe as Myth," *Essays in Criticism:*
A Quarterly Journal of Literary Criticism (April 1951). Reprinted
in *The Arts in Society,* ed. Robert N. Wilson (Englewood Cliffs, NJ:
Prentice-Hall, 1964), 150, 152

Questions for Discussion and Further Research

1. What does Watt say about Faust, Don Juan, and Don Quixote as mythic figures?
2. How does Robinson Crusoe relate to "three essential themes of modern civilization"?
3. How does myth work, according to Watt? Do you agree with him? Justify your position.
4. Do you think Crusoe's values have particular appeal to Americans? Explain your answer.
5. Define "paradigmatic" hero. Are there any new paradigmatic heroes? Who are they?
6. Who are the dominant heroes and heroines in the media today? What values do they represent?

It's hard to classify a novel such as *Robinson Crusoe*, since it is quite obviously more than just a story meant to entertain young children. What it is, Watt argues, is a formative myth that reflects important cultural values. Watt suggests that there are three great myths of Western civilization:

Faust	Single-minded pursuit of knowledge
Don Juan	Single-minded pursuit of women
Don Quixote	Single-minded pursuit of chivalric ideal

Robinson Crusoe is similar to these culture heroes in that his life, also, is based on the single-minded pursuit—that of achievement and enterprise (business success). The story, Watt suggests, deals with three important themes found in modern civilization: back to nature, the dignity of labor, and the pursuit of economic gain. It was Crusoe's greed, let us remember, that was the cause of his ending up on the desert island, where he was to spend so many years by himself.

Crusoe is best seen as a symbolic culture hero whose adventures reflect these three themes and who also teaches readers to adopt these values. We tend to identify with heroes and heroines in stories we read (or see in the movies or on television or in videos), and thus there is good reason to suggest that Crusoe is a paradigmatic hero, whose mind frame, behavior, and values become important to us—even though we may not be conscious that this is taking place.

An interesting process has occurred, Watt asserts. It is the public that has turned the story of Robinson Crusoe into a myth because the story reflects, in such profound ways, the public's deeply held but unconscious beliefs and values. "It is not an author but a society that metamorphoses a story into a myth" ("Robinson Crusoe as Myth," 152), Watt says, by keeping elements in the story that its unconscious needs require and discarding everything else. Writers have some idea of what they are doing when they write a novel, but they cannot anticipate the way the public will react to their efforts. Some stories strike a responsive chord, and the task of the literary critic and media analyst is to figure out why this chord was struck.

Watt offers us an interesting perspective by which to analyze heroes and heroines, and villains as well, in popular culture. The question we must ask, when dealing with these figures—especially the very successful ones—is, what unconscious needs do they satisfy? Why are people attracted to them? How do they help people deal with unrecognized or unconscious elements of their personalities? And what do they reflect about the cultures and societies in which we find them? Stories such as *Robinson Crusoe* and other texts (rock songs, rap songs, films, television shows, television commercials, videos, and one could go only endlessly here) are, as we shall see, actually very complicated works. When you add the way audiences respond to these works, the task of the culture and media analyst becomes that much more difficult.

Robinson Crusoe

Robinson Crusoe as Myth

29 ▸ Fairy Tales and the Psyche

O n an overt level fairy tales teach little about the specific conditio... ᴜᵢ ᴍᴇ in modern mass society; these tales were created long before it came into being. But more can be learned from them about the inner problems of human beings, and of the right solutions to their predicaments in any society, than from any other type of story within a child's comprehension. Since the child at every moment of his life is exposed to the society in which he lives, he will certainly learn to cope with its conditions, provided his inner resources permit him to do so. . . .

Through the centuries (if not millennia) during which, in their retelling, fairy tales became ever more refined, they came to convey at the same time overt and covert meanings—came to speak simultaneously to all levels of the human personality, communicating in a manner which reaches the uneducated mind of the child as well as that of the sophisticated adult. Applying the psychoanalytic model of the human personality, fairy tales carry important messages to the conscious, the preconscious, and the unconscious mind, on whatever level each is functioning at the time. By dealing with universal human problems, particularly those which occupy the child's mind, these stories speak to his budding ego and encourage its development, while at the same time relieving preconscious and unconscious pressures. As the stories unfold, they give conscious credence and body to id pressures and show ways to satisfy these that are in line with ego and superego requirements.

They speak about his severe inner pressures in a way that the child unconsciously understands, and—without belittling the most serious struggles which growing up entails—offer examples of both temporary and permanent solutions to pressing difficulties.

— Bruno Bettelheim, *The Uses of Enchantment: The Meaning and Importance of Fairy Tales* (New York, Knopf, 1976), 5, 6

Questions for Discussion and Further Research

1. How does Bettelheim explain the importance that fairy tales have for young children?
2. What special qualities do fairy tales have that enable them to work the way they do?
3. Does Bettelheim's psychoanalytic approach seem far-fetched or useful? Defend your position.
4. Compare myths and fairy tales. Why does Bettelheim suggest that myths are bad for children?

Fairy tales have an ancient lineage, but unlike the fertility goddess–Miss America figure, they continue to play in important role in our lives. As Bettelheim points out, these tales come down to us from ancient times, and over the millennia they have been modified by their tellers until they have attained a form in which they play an important role in helping children deal with the psychological pressures they face in growing up. According to Bettelheim, these tales are quite different from conventional children's stories and from stories about mythic heroes.

The differences between mythic heroes and heroines and those found in fairy tales are shown in the chart that follows (adapted from my book *Narratives in Media, Popular Culture and Everyday Life* [Berger 1997]).

Myths	*Fairy Tales*
Direct, didactic	Indirect
Gods and demigods, superhuman characters	Ordinary heroes and heroines
Particularized characters	Typical, generalized characters
Majestic presentation	Simple presentation
Demands made on readers	No demands made on readers
The unique	The typical
Tragic endings (often)	Happy endings
Pessimistic	Optimistic ("they all lived happily ever after")
Superego is dominant	Ego integration depicted

What myths do, Bettelheim argues, is show idealized characters who are dominated by the demands of their superegos. Fairy tales, on the other hand, show an ego integration that makes possible the satisfaction of unrecognized, unconscious id desires felt by the child. Bettelheim's discussion here draws on

Fairy Tales and the Psyche

Freud's analysis of the psyche as being divided into three parts: the id, the ego, and the superego, and his theory about the three levels of the conscious in the human psyche: consciousness, the subconscious, and the unconscious. These topics were dealt with in chapter 4 in my discussion of the selection from Freud.

Fairy Tale

Why kids want to hear the same story over + over again

helps to deal with pressures in kid's lives

Bettelheim, taking a psychoanalytic perspective, assumes that children experience many different difficulties and challenges as they grow up and argues that fairy tales have a unique ability to speak to children in remarkable ways and to help them deal with their difficulties in positive ways. That explains why children often ask their parents to read a certain fairy tale over and over again. The reason children act this way, Bettelheim would suggest, is because that particular fairy tale helps children, at a given point in their development, deal with pressures they feel or other kinds of problems they face.

The Freudian psychoanalytic model of human personality suggests that all through life we face challenges and have to overcome difficulties of various kinds that come our way. When we are children, fairy tales help us. But when we are older, when we are more mature, what do we use to cope with problems and difficulties we face? One thing we use, I would suggest, is humor—which pervades our media. We are also helped by therapy and, for some people, what might be described as "better living through chemistry," which involves everything from alcoholic beverages to various drugs our doctors prescribe for us (and some they don't prescribe for us).

Fairytales → kids

*Therapy
drugs
alc.
humor → adults*

30 Hot and Cool Media

There is a basic principle that distinguishes a hot medium like radio from a cool one like the telephone, or a hot medium like the movie from a cool one like TV. A hot medium is one that extends one single sense in "high definition." High definition is the state of being well filled with data. A photograph is visually "high definition." A cartoon is "low definition," simply because very little visual information is provided. Telephone is a cool medium, or one of low definition, because the ear is given a meager amount of information. And speech is a cool medium of low definition, because so little is given and so much has to be filled in by the listener. On the other hand, hot media do not leave so much to be filled in or completed by the audience. Naturally, therefore, a hot medium like the radio has very different effects on the user from a cool medium like the telephone. . . .

In terms of the theme of media hot and cold, backward countries are cool and we are hot. The "city slicker" is hot, and the rustic is cool. But in terms of the reversal of procedures and values in the electric age, the past mechanical one was hot, and we of the TV age are cool. The waltz was a hot, fast mechanical dance suited to the industrial time in its moods of pomp and circumstance. In contrast, the Twist is a cool, involved and chatty form of improvised gesture. The jazz of the period of the hot new media of movie and radio was hot jazz. Yet jazz of itself tends to be a casual dialogue form of dance quite lacking in the repetitive and mechanical form of the waltz.

— Marshall McLuhan, *Understanding Media: The Extensions of Man*
(New York: McGraw-Hill, 1956), 22–23, 27

Questions for Discussion and Further Research

1. How does McLuhan characterize "hot" and "cool" media? Which are "hot" and which are "cool"?
2. What are the social and political implications of these two kinds of media?
3. What does McLuhan mean by "definition," and what roles does it play in his ideas about media?
4. Why does McLuhan describe himself as a satirist?
5. Why do you think McLuhan was interested in "hidden levels of meaning" found in pop culture?
6. Is the Internet hot or cool? Justify your position, based on McLuhan's ideas about hot and cool media.

The late Marshall McLuhan was famous for any number of statements and ideas. One of his most famous (or notorious) was "the medium is the message." In his book Understanding Media, McLuhan developed another important concept that classified certain media as "hot" and other media as "cool." We can see the differences between the two kinds of media in the chart below. I have taken the items in this chart from the material in the McLuhan selection and other sections of Understanding Media as well as from the implications of some of McLuhan's ideas:

Hot media	Cool media
High definition	Low definition
Filled with data	Little data provided
Extends a single sense	No sense is dominant
Photograph	Cartoon
Radio	Telephone
First World countries	Third World countries
Films	Television
City slicker	Rustic
Past mechanical age	Present TV age
Lecture	Seminar

It's important to classify media because hot and cool media have different social and political effects. A hot medium like radio provides a great deal more data or information than a cool one like the telephone, and the effects of these different kinds of media are also different. Thus, a hot medium like radio is good for shaping the behavior of large groups of people, while a cool medium like the telephone—or, in its newest incarnation, the mobile telephone (which can now take photographs, make short videos, send text messages, and so on)—has different social effects, creating "smart mobs" as Howard Rheingold points out in his selection in chapter 36. If the mobile telephone creates "smart mobs," then we can infer that the radio creates "dumb mobs," who act on the basis of their passions, which become inflamed by the "theatrical representations" (as Gustave Le Bon puts it) carried on radio.

Marshall McLuhan was very popular in the sixties and seventies and then more or less faded from view. In recent years, as our interest in the role of digital media has become more pronounced, many of McLuhan's ideas are being rediscovered, and he is now seen as a visionary theorist by many communications and media scholars. A remarkable biography of McLuhan by Donald Theall, *The Virtual Marshall McLuhan*, quotes a letter from McLuhan to a Canadian poet, Michael Hornyasnky, in which McLuhan describes himself: "Most of my writing is Menippean satire, presenting the actual surface of the world we live in as a ludicrous image" (2001, 63).

Theall suggests, then, that we should see McLuhan in a new light. Theall writes,

> From his insistence on his role as poet, satirist, "pattern watcher," and sci-fi predictor of the future (because of his living in the present and loving the past) capable of major contributions to our understanding of the information society, a new figure of McLuhan emerges which demands his revaluation as a twentieth-century poet and satirist concerned with probing rather than theorizing about communication, culture, and technology in the emerging technoculture. (2001, 66)

Theall describes how McLuhan became interested in media and popular culture. McLuhan had become frustrated trying to teach young college students how to analyze English poetry and came to the conclusion that applying the critical methods of analysis he had learned at Cambridge University from the Cambridge school of literary interpretation to the front pages of newspapers, to advertisements, and to comic strips made more sense.

As Theall writes,

> This new approach to the study of popular culture and popular art forms led to his first major move towards new media and communication and eventually resulted in his first book, *The Mechanical Bride*, which some consider to be one of the founding documents of early cultural studies. . . . *The Bride* illustrated yet another aspect of the ongoing McLuhanesque approach to cultural phenomena—the satiric use of wit and the comic as a mode of "tweaking" hidden levels of meaning

and complexity from material that seems to be relatively simple—
Blondie, Li'l Abner, the front page of a Hearst tabloid, ads for caskets,
laundry soap, or stockings. (2001, 4, 5)

This satirical approach, Theall adds, was to inform McLuhan's work for the rest
of his career. *The Mechanical Bride* should be seen as a parody of the ad styles and
pop culture world that McLuhan was investigating—as a critic, before he
became a media theorist.

I can recall once discussing McLuhan's ideas in one of my book manu-
scripts. A professor, who was asked by my publisher to evaluate my manuscript,
was outraged that I "wasted" any time on McLuhan. I have to say that I was
shocked by the vehemence of this professor's response to my discussion of
McLuhan. Ironically, McLuhan has now become one of the theorists whose
ideas are of most interest to scholars concerned with the way our digital media
are developing and affecting American and other cultures and societies. The fact
that McLuhan was a satirist suggests that in some respects he was "putting us all
on," so to speak, which means he also must be considered as a postmodernist figure, among other things. Postmodernism is the subject I deal with in the chapter that follows.

31 ▶ The Impact of Postmodernism

Premonitions of the future, catastrophic or redemptive, have been replaced by senses of the end of this or that (the end of ideology, art, or social class; the "crisis" of Leninism, social democracy, or the welfare state, etc. etc.); taken together, all of these perhaps constitute what is increasingly called postmodernism. . . . As the word itself suggests, this break is most often related to notions of the waning or extinction of the hundred-year-old modern movement (or to its ideological or aesthetic repudiation). Thus abstract expressionism in painting, existentialism in philosophy, the final forms of representation in the novel, the films of the great *auteurs,* or the modernist school of poetry . . . all are now seen as the final, extraordinary flowering of a high-modernist impulse which is spent and exhausted with them. The enumeration of what follows, then, at once becomes empirical, chaotic, and heterogeneous. Andy Warhol and pop art, but also photorealism, and beyond it, the "new expressionism"; the moment, in music, of John Cage, but also the synthesis of classical and "popular" styles found in composers like Phil Glass and Terry Riley, and also punk and new wave rock (the Beatles and the Stones now standing as the high-modernist moment of that more recent and rapidly evolving tradition). . . .

[There is] one fundamental feature of all the postmodernisms enumerated above: namely the effacement in them of the older (essentially high-modernist) frontier between high culture and so-called mass or commercial culture. . . . The postmodernists have, in fact, been fascinated precisely by this whole "degraded" landscape of schlock and kitsch, of TV series and *Reader's Digest* culture, of advertising and motels, of the late show and the grade-B Hollywood film, of so-called paraliterature, with its airport paperback categories of the gothic and the romance, the popular biography, the murder mystery, and the science fiction or fantasy novel. . . .

— Fredric Jameson, *Postmodernism, or, The Cultural Logic of Late Capitalism* (Durham, NC: Duke University Press, 1995), 1–3

Questions for Discussion and Further Research

1. What examples does Jameson offer of modernism and postmodernism?
2. What are the dominant features of modernism and postmodernism?
3. What does "incredulity toward metanarratives" mean? Why is it important?
4. Jameson links postmodernism with capitalism and consumer cultures. Explain his thinking.
5. Do you think you've been affected by "the degraded landscape" Jameson writes about? Explain.

According to many postmodernist thinkers, an important change has taken place in American society since around 1960, when an aesthetic style and approach to culture and life known as modernism was replaced by one known as postmodernism. Jean-François Lyotard described postmodernism as "incredulity toward metanarratives" (1984), by which he meant a rejection of the grand, all-encompassing systems of thought (as found in religions, philosophy, and political ideologies such as Marxism) in favor of many different narratives that vie for favor. We see striking differences between the two in architecture. Modernist architecture, as exemplified in the Bauhaus and buildings of Mies Van Der Rohe, is very formal, unified, and simple. Postmodernist buildings, on the other hand, are eclectic and often have a number of different architectural styles in them. The pastiche, in which different items (and styles) are combined, becomes the basic model for culture.

In the chart below, I list and contrast a number of the basic attributes of modernism and postmodernism. This chart reflects the ideas of many commentators on postmodern culture as well as Jameson's notions about what we find in postmodernist societies—though he offers a different explanation of what postmodernism represents:

Moderism	Postmodernism
Master (meta) narratives	Local narratives
Unified style	Fragmented style
Harmonious	Eclectic
Hierarchical	Anarchical
Separates high culture over pop culture	Merges high culture and pop culture
Abstract expressionism	Pop art, photorealism
Classical music styles	Punk
"Serious" art	Schlock art

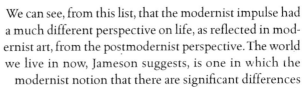

We can see, from this list, that the modernist impulse had a much different perspective on life, as reflected in modernist art, from the postmodernist perspective. The world we live in now, Jameson suggests, is one in which the modernist notion that there are significant differences between so-called high or elite art and popular culture is rejected, so nowadays anything goes. He asserts that we now live in a world with a "degraded" postmodern landscape full of schlock art and kitsch in which art forms such as television series, motel design, and advertising are dominant.

The subtitle of Jameson's book is significant: *The Cultural Logic of Late Capitalism*. He argues, in his book, that what we call postmodernism is best thought of as a stage of "late capitalism," a new form of capitalism characterized by the development of consumer cultures and by the degraded postmodernist landscape, as he describes things, that comes with it.

In the selection in the following chapter, on the "postmodern eye" by Jack Solomon, we find another perspective on postmodernism. He deals with media and the loss of narrative structure and the loss of a sense of center in the postmodern worldview.

32 ▶ The Postmodern Eye

Postmodernism represents a new mode of perception fostered by an age of instant communication by radio, cinema and, most importantly, by TV. Viewing the world as a television camera views it, the postmodern eye reduces the length and breadth of experience to a two-dimensional spectacle, to a carnival of arresting images and seductive surfaces. Like the nightly news, whose quick camera cuts can juxtapose images of international violence with pitches for fabric softeners and headache remedies, the postmodern experience is best described as a perceptual montage. Gazing upon the world as if it were one vast variety show, the postmodern eye perceives the course of human events as a narrativeless and nonsensical series of skits, as one long episode of "Monty Python." . . .

A narrative . . . is very much like a myth, taking the disorganized stuff of experience and casting it in a meaningful frame. As Aristotle put it in "Poetics," the West's first major work of narrative analysis, the plot, or mythos, of a story is what gives it shape, endowing the particularity of human experience with a universal significance. . . . In essence, that's what narratives have always been for: to create meaning in the face of meaningless, to make sense of the senselessness of the world in which we live and die. . . .

In the postmodern worldview, narrative has lost its sacred power. The semiotic significance of this loss is profound, for by rejecting the traditional narratives of the West, the postmodern myth has rejected the centering structures that have long given meaning to human history. At the postmodern center there is only a void, which is the same as saying that there is no center to the postmodern worldview. . . . Life is nothing more than a decentered, narrativeless course of waiting for death—or for a nonexistent God who never comes.

— Jack Solomon, *The Signs of Our Times: The Secret Meanings of
Everyday Life* (New York: Perennial, 1990), 212, 214–216

Questions for Discussion and Further Research

1. How does Solomon characterize postmodernism?
2. Compare Solomon and Jameson on postmodernism. Do they differ? Explain your answer.
3. What does Solomon mean by "perpetual montage"? What role does it play in our lives?
4. Why, in postmodern societies, has narrative lost its "sacred" power? What impact does this have?
5. What does it mean to be "decentered"? What role do the media play in this matter?
6. Investigate "simulacra" and "hyperreality" and see how they relate to postmodernism.

Jack Solomon explains the significance of postmodernism to us in terms of its impact on the way we see the world, through what he calls a "postmodern eye." His argument is that as a result of the power and ubiquity of television and our other mass media, postmodernism, in destroying our master narratives in philosophy and other areas of human thought, has destroyed what we have used to give meaning to life—our narratives. Life has lost its center, he suggests, and our lives in postmodern societies are "decentered."

Narratives have the function of imposing order on chaos, of creating meaning from the blur of events and signs in which our lives are immersed. If you take away these narratives, life then becomes a series of random events, none of which have any more importance than any others (since there is no narrative or story to give events meaning). In traditional narratives, there is a plot that gives events significance and enables us to understand their meaning. In a narrative-less existence, or one in which there are no agreed upon notions of plot and story and everyone is making up his or her own story, nothing has any importance, and life then becomes "meaningless," by which Solomon means robbed of meaning.

Solomon argues that postmodernism represents an attempt to adapt to the conditions of modern life, dominated as it is by our media and new digital technologies. In the selection by Lewis Carroll in this book, Alice (of *Alice in Wonderland* fame) asks Humpty Dumpty about the way he uses words, and he explains that he uses words any way he wants to use them. It all boils down to who will be master, he says. That is the question we ask about the world we live in now, except we are dealing with machines, devices, new technologies, and their relationship to human beings. The answer that the postmodernists offer us, with their talk about simulacra and hyperrealities, is not very encouraging.

33 Mind and Media

All of us, no matter how irresolute we are, like to think that we reign supreme in our own consciousness, that we are masters of what our minds accept or reject. Since the Soul is not much mentioned any more, except by priests, poets, and pop musicians, the last refuge a man can take from the catastrophic world at large seems to be his own mind. Where else can he expect to withstand the daily siege, if not within himself? Even under the conditions of totalitarian rule, where no one can fancy any more that his home is his castle, the mind of the individual is considered a kind of last citadel and hotly defended though this imaginary fortress may have been long since taken over by an ingenious enemy.

No illusion is more stubbornly upheld than the sovereignty of the mind. It is a good example of the impact of philosophy on people who ignore it. . . . We might do worse, I think, than dust off the admirably laconic statement which one of our classics made more than a century ago: "What is going on in our minds has always been, and will always be, a product of society." This is a comparatively recent insight. . . .

The mind-making industry is really a product of the last hundred years. It has developed at such a pace, and assumed such varied forms, that it has outgrown our understanding and our control. Our current discussion of the "media" seems to suffer from severe theoretical limitations. Newsprint, films, television, public relations tend to be evaluated separately, in terms of their specific technologies, conditions, and possibilities. Every new branch of the industry starts off a new crop of theories. Hardly anyone seems to be aware of the phenomenon as a whole: the industrialization of the human mind.

— Hans Magnus Enzenberger, *The Consciousness Industry: On Literature, Politics & the Media* (New York: Seabury, 1974), 3

Questions for Discussion and Further Research

1. What arguments does Enzenberger make about the sovereignty of the mind?
2. Support this statement: "What is going on in our minds is a product of society." Then attack it.
3. What role do the media play in the "industrialization" of the mind?
4. What did Durkheim say about the relationship between individuals and society?
5. Has your mind has been "invaded" by the media, with "illusions" of freedom? Justify your answer.
6. Which is more important in socialization: parents, peers, priests, or pop culture? Explain your answer.

The mind has been "industrialized," argues Hans Magnus Enzenberger, which means that our notion that we completely control the contents of our minds is an illusion. We go about, blindly believing that our thoughts are our own, when in reality, Enzenberger argues, our minds have been "industrialized," and the contents of our minds are "and will always be a product of society." This is a topic that we have encountered before and that pervades many discussions of communication: What is the relationship that exists between our individual minds and society at large?

The French sociologist Emile Durkheim argued that human beings are both individuals and also social beings and that we exist in society, and at the same time society exists within us. The field of study known as the sociology of knowledge deals with this matter. Where is knowledge to be located? Individuals may have ideas, but where do they get them? Sociologists argue that thought is social, and while individuals think, what they think is heavily influenced by what others have thought before them. As Karl Mannheim explained in his book *Ideology and Utopia*, "Those who talk most about human freedom are those who are actually most blindly subject to social determination, inasmuch as they do not in most cases suspect the profound degree to which their conduct is determined by their interests" (1936, 48).

Thus, Enzenberger argues that most of our discussions of the power of media are simplistic and tend to focus on particular attributes of specific media without recognizing that something more profound has happened, and as a result of the rapid development of the mass media: our minds have been "industrialized," which suggests they are a product, a commodity, not too far removed from other industrialized products such as toothpaste or teacups. What the media are, in truth, are "mind-making" industries, and their power is more insidious because most people go around with the fallacious idea that their minds are "citadels" that cannot be breached by the media (or anything else) while, in fact, that is exactly what has happened.

One interesting question arises here: If our minds are industrialized social products, where did Enzenberger get this notion? Where do any new ideas come from? The answer seems to be that some individuals are not socialized as much or as "correctly" as others and thus can observe phenomena more dispassionately and more honestly. Most people, Enzenberger suggests, go around with the illusion that their minds cannot be invaded by the media while, in actuality, their minds are now industrialized ones in which this idea that our minds are inviolate has been implanted.

34 ▸ Cybertexts and Video Games

Behind each of the singularistic concepts of sender, message, and receiver in traditional communication theory there is a complex continuum of positions, or functions. (These are not related to Roman Jakobson's [1960] communicative functions.) When I fire a laser gun in a computer game such as *Space Invader* [*sic*], where, and what, am "I"? Am I the sender or the receiver? I am certainly part of the medium, so perhaps I am the message. Compare Umberto Eco's statement that "what one usually calls message is rather a text, a network of different messages depending on different codes" (1976, 141). If this definition is applied to a computer game program such as *Space Invader* [*sic*], it becomes nontrivial to attribute these concepts to specific communicative positions: just as the game becomes a text for the user at the time of playing, so, it can be argued, does the user become a text for the game, since they exchange and react to each other's messages according to a set of codes. The game plays the user and there is no message apart from the play.

This epistemological problem comes into focus every time the known media increase in number and complexity. The step from speech to phonetic writing that took place some six thousand years ago in the Middle East is not merely an expansion of the reach of language in time and space, or a splitting up of language into two different media, or a new mode of graphical expression, but an event that creates an awareness of language as something other than its written or spoken realization. To write is not the same as to speak; listening and reading are different activities, with different positions in the communicative topology.

— Espen J. Aarseth, *Cybertext: Perspectives on Ergodic Literature* (Baltimore: Johns Hopkins University Press, 1997), 162

Questions for Discussion and Further Research

1. What does Aarseth say about the relationship between players and video games?
2. Support the statement "video games play people." Define "video game."
3. How do Jakobson's and Umberto Eco's arguments fit into Aarseth's notions?
4. How do video games affect our notions about authorship?
5. Why are video games so addictive? What implications does their addictive nature have?
6. What video games have you played? What aspects of each game are most appealing to you? Why?

Aarseth raises an interesting question here about video games. Do people play games or do games play people? Where, in the traditional model of communication, with senders and messages or texts and receivers, does the player of a video game fit? The game, he suggests, is a text for the user (that is, game player) but, at the same time, the user becomes a text for the game. This is because, Aarseth explains, they exchange and react to each other's messages. And, he adds, "There is no message apart from the play."

Video games, then, makes us think about the relationship that exists between authors and readers or creators and users. The old notion that there is an author who creates a work and a reader who reads this work has been attacked by reader-response theorists (also known as reception theorists). Readers, these theorists argue, help bring a work into being. A novel is an inert object without a reader, so things aren't simple when it comes to reading books. Video games further complicate the matter of distinguishing between readers/players and authors/creators—since players help determine how a game is to progress and thus, in a sense, transform the text.

Aarseth, elsewhere in his book, defines ergodic art as works that contain the rules for their use and that have certain requirements that enable us to distinguish between successful and unsuccessful users. In video games, players have an important role in the outcome of the game. There is some question in my mind as to whether video game players have an illusion that their input is all-important, since everything they do has been coded into the game and a player's options are limited. But most certainly there are options and what a player does has certain consequences, so games do not proceed along the linear line that a literary work of fiction does. And in video games, the player becomes the main character.

As video games evolve and become more and more like films, players become more and more like movie stars, and their adventures in these games become more realistic and exciting. We can understand, then, why video games are so addictive. When the pleasures (sexual and otherwise) of video games become much greater than those offered by real life, what will happen? That is a question that people are beginning to worry about. The digital revolution that enables us to listen to whatever music we want when we want it, that created the computer, and that has freed us from being tied to phones in our homes and makes possible "smart mobs" may also be undermining our social fabric and eventually even our identities. Perhaps Aarseth is correct and these video games are playing us—but how the game they are playing with us will end is hard to predict.

35 ▸ Digital Media

Media critic Neil Postman wrote an homage to Aldous Huxley in his introduction to the Voyager electronic book that paired Postman's *Amusing Ourselves to Death* with Huxley's *Brave New World.* When 1984 came and went, Americans congratulated themselves on the fact that Orwell's Big Brother had not materialized in the West. But what people missed, of course, was that Huxley's infinitely darker vision had come true. As Postman put it, in *Brave New World,* Huxley saw a time coming when "people will come to love their oppression, to adore the technologies that undo their capacities to think." In Huxley's fiction, it's the drug soma; in Postman's analysis of our society, it's television.

Given the fact that I generally address my remarks to audiences composed precisely of those involved in the development of new digital technologies, they understand this reference to soma's addictive power. They understand, at least subliminally, that when immersive games, interactive television, and on-line entertainment come into their own, they will be incredibly powerful. (And in the service of those who don't mind having people controlled.) Anyone with eight- or nine-year-old children at home who watches them play in front of a game screen for half a day can attest to the attractions that even our still quite primitive machines offer. . . .

My theme boils down to two questions: What are we going to use these technologies for? What kind of society do we want to live in? . . . If we do not ask the questions, there is no doubt in my mind that we are going to end up in a bad place.

— Bob Stein, "'We Could Be Better Ancestors Than This': Ethics and
    First Principles for the Art of the Digital Age," in *The Digital
    Dialectic: New Essays on New Media,* ed. Peter Lunenfeld
    (Cambridge: MIT Press: 1999), 204–205

Questions for Discussion and Further Research

1. What argument does Stein make about the power of television?
2. In what ways is television like the Huxley drug "soma"?
3. Why are immersive games, interactive television, and online entertainment so powerful?
4. What questions does Stein ask about technology? What answers would you give? Why?
5. Investigate and define: "immersive," "digital," "video game," "teledildonics."

Bob Stein approaches television and the new digital media that are being developed from a moral point of view. He asks us how we are going to use our media technologies, and a question allied to that, what kind of society do we want to create? His essay is similar to Enzenberger's in that Stein asserts that Americans were mistaken when they concluded that George Orwell's dark vision of a totalitarian society dominated by Big Brother did not materialize in 1984. What had happened is that Aldous Huxley's "darker vision" of a society dominated by the "technologies that undo their capacities to think" had already been realized, and thus Americans were, in Neil Postman's terms, "entertaining themselves to death."

Stein focuses his attention on video games and other immersive digital technologies and the effects they have on people. Players easily become addicted to the successively greater gratifications that these immersive games offer, as anyone with an eight- or nine-year-old child recognizes. The new multiplayer online games are even worse and have had traumatic effects on the lives of some individuals who became addicted to them and who neglected other aspects of their lives—their wives, their children, and their jobs, in some instances, with calamitous results. These games are now relatively primitive. What will happen, Stein asks, when they develop to a higher degree? What will the people who control these new immersive technologies use them for? That is a question that has chilling implications.

For example, let's consider our sexual needs. In his 1992 book, *Virtual Reality,* Howard Rheingold describes the possibilities new technologies offer us for virtual sex in his chapter "Teledildonics and Beyond." He writes,

> The first fully functional teledildonics system will be a communication device, not a sex machine. You probably will not use erotic telepresence technology in order to have sexual experiences with machines. Thirty years from now, when portable telediddlers become ubiquitous, most people will use them to have sexual experiences with other *people,* at a

distance, in combinations and configurations undreamed of by precy-bernetic voluptuaries. Through a marriage of virtual reality technology and telecommunications networks, you will be able to reach out and touch someone—or an entire population—in ways humans have never before experienced. Or so the scenario goes. (345)

This new kind of telecommunicated sex would be facilitated by people wearing body suits full of sensory devices (not yet in existence) having telesex with one another.

Stein's questions about moral judgments by people who create and control new technologies are ones that we continue to wrestle with. Is having sex with machines something we should look forward to? Will some electronic variation of Huxley's drug "soma" be created to dominate our lives and, if Rheingold is correct, perhaps even our sexuality? Is all this something we should look forward to, or should we fight this kind of thing with all our energy?

36 ▶ Smart Mobs

On a Spring afternoon in the year 2000 I began to notice people on the streets of Tokyo staring at their mobile phones instead of talking to them. The sight of this behavior, now commonplace in much of the world, triggered a sensation I had experienced a few times before—the instant recognition that a technology is going to change my life in ways I can scarcely imagine. Since then, the practice of exchanging short text messages via mobile telephones has led to the eruption of subcultures in Europe and Asia. At least one government has fallen, in part because of the way people used text messaging.

Adolescent mating rituals, political activism, and corporate management styles have mutated in unexpected ways.

I've learned that "texting" is only a small harbinger of more profound changes to come over the next ten years. My media moment at Shibuya Crossing was only my first encounter with a phenomenon I've come to call "smart mobs." When I learned to recognize the signs, I began to see them everywhere—from Napster to electronic bridge tolls.

The other pieces of the puzzle are all around us now, but haven't joined together yet. The radio chips designed to replace bar codes on manufactured objects are part of it. Wireless Internet nodes in cafes, hotels, and neighborhoods are part of it. Millions of people who lend their computers to the search for extraterrestrial intelligence are part of it. The way buyers and sellers rate each other on Internet auction site eBay is part of it. At least one key global business question is part of it—why is the Japanese company DoCoMo profiting from enhanced wireless Internet services while US and European mobile telephony operators struggle to avoid failure?

When you piece together these different technological, economic, and social components, the result is an infrastructure that makes certain kinds of human actions possible that were never possible before: The killer apps of tomorrow's mobile infocom industry won't be hardware devices or software programs but social practices. The most far-reaching changes will come, as they often do, from the kinds of relationships, enterprises, communities and markets that the infrastructure makes possible.

— Howard Rheingold, *Smart Mobs* (New York: Perseus, 2003), xi–xii

Questions for Discussion and Further Research

1. What does Rheingold say about the impact of text messaging on society and politics?
2. What other profound changes caused by technology does Rheingold talk about?
3. How does Rheingold define and explain "smart mobs"? How can a mob be smart?
4. What does Rheingold say about technology and social practices?
5. Do you use text messaging? If so, how do you use it? What role does it play in your social life?

Howard Rheingold, one of the most astute observers of the role new technologies are playing in contemporary culture, offers us a new image of crowds—quite different from the one Gustave Le Bon offered us in 1895. (His ideas are discussed in the next chapter.) Rheingold's notion of "smart mobs" is based on implications that stem from the technology of the mobile phone, and of one particular feature of these new phones—their ability to send text messages to other people with mobile phones.

As Rheingold describes his experience, it was a kind of epiphany, a moment of insight that struck him at a particular moment, the year 2000, in a particular place, the Shibuya Crossing in Tokyo. It was at that moment and in that place that he noticed people staring at their phones instead of talking into them. He realized, then, that something rather profound had taken place, as a result of this new technology. We could say that at that moment, Rheingold saw the thumb as now taking an important place, along with the voice, in the scheme of things, since it is with thumbs that people send text messages on their phones. In many cases, text message senders don't even have to look at the phone keyboard—they are similar to touch typists in that respect. And in many cases, they multitask: have a conversation with one person and send a text message to someone else.

But this technological revolution is most important, Rheingold suggests, in terms of the societal changes it will engender. It is the new social practices that text messaging is bringing into being that are the real significance of this phenomenon, creating, in Rheingold's terms, "smart mobs." Smart mobs can be thought of as groups of people who organize themselves for social and political purposes through their common use of cell phones and text messaging. The social and political implications that will result from such smart mobs have yet to work themselves out, but there is good reason to believe that they will be profound.

37 How Crowds Think

Just as is the case with respect to persons in whom the reasoning power is absent, the figurative imagination of crowds is very powerful, very active, and very susceptible of being keenly impressed. The images evoked in their mind by a personage, an event, an accident, are almost as lifelike as the reality. Crowds are to some extent in the position of the sleeper whose reason, suspended for the time being, allows the arousing in his mind of images of extreme intensity which would quickly be dissipated could they be submitted to the action of reflection. . . .

Appearances have always played a much more important part than reality in history, where the unreal is always of greater moment than the real. Crowds being only capable of thinking in images are only to be impressed by images. It is only images that terrify or attract them and become motives of action.

For this reason theatrical representations, in which the image is shown in its most clearly visible shape, always have an enormous influence on crowds. Bread and spectacular shows constituted for the plebeians of ancient Rome the ideal of happiness, and they asked for nothing more. Throughout the successive ages this ideal has scarcely varied. Nothing has a greater effect on the imagination of crowds of every category than theatrical representations. The entire audience experiences at the same time the same emotions, and if these emotions are not at once transformed into acts, it is because the most unconscious spectator cannot ignore the fact that he has laughed or wept over imaginary adventures. Sometimes, however, the sentiments suggested by the images are so strong that they tend, like habitual suggestions, to transform themselves into act.

— Gustave Le Bon, *The Crowd: A Study of the Popular Mind* (New York: Viking Press, 1960), 67–68

Questions for Discussion and Further Research

1. What does Le Bon say about the relation between crowds and individuals?
2. What role do "theatrical representations" play in Le Bon's argument?
3. What does he say about the way audiences experience theatrical representations? Do you agree?
4. How does he justify his assertion that appearances are more important than reality? Is he correct?
5. Explain Iser's "reception theory" and discuss its implications for our media usage.

Gustave Le Bon's book *The Crowd* is generally considered to be one of the classics of sociological theory. It was originally published in 1895 and was reprinted in 1960, with an introduction by a distinguished sociologist, Robert K. Merton. Like the postmodernist culture theorist Jean Baudrillard, Le Bon was also interested in images—and, more precisely, in the way that "theatrical representations" and what we would now call mass-mediated culture, such as film, video, and television, influence crowds, audiences, and, by extension, public opinion. We use the term *theater* now to cover all kinds of different phenomena. Think, for example, of the Democratic and Republican conventions, which are generally described as "political theater." The aim of the conventions, designed for maximum effectiveness on television, is to influence voters.

Appearances, Le Bon tells us, have always been more important than reality. This notion anticipates in very broad terms Baudrillard's ideas about simulacra. Le Bon believes that an audience "experiences at the same time the same emotions" from theatrical representations, a theory very similar to one that used to be popular, known as the "hypodermic needle theory" of media. It asserted that everyone in an audience got the same message from the texts they were exposed to—songs that they listened to on the radio, books that they read, texts that they watched on video or television, films that they went to, or plays that they saw. This theory is no longer accepted, having been displanted by what is called "reader-response" or "reception" theory.

Wolfgang Iser, a German media theorist, offers a classic statement of this theory. He writes,

> The text as such offers different "schematized views" through which the subject matter of the work can come to light, but the actual bringing of light is an action of *Konkretisation*. If this is so, then the literary work has two poles, which we might call the artistic and the aesthetic: the artistic refers to the text created by the author, and the aesthetic to the realiza-

tion accomplished by the reader. From this polarity it follows that the literary work cannot be completely identical with the text, or with the realization of the text, but in fact must lie halfway between the two. The work is more than the text, for the text only takes life when it is realized and furthermore the realization is by no means independent of the individual disposition of the reader—though this in turn is acted upon by the different patterns of the text. (1988, 212)

In this passage, Iser is dealing with literary works, but we can apply his ideas to deal with any mass-mediated text. When we watch a mass-mediated text such as a film or television program, we interpret it on the basis of our education, social background, and knowledge base. Nevertheless, even though reception theory argues that we all interpret a text differently, in certain respects we tend to interpret them in similar ways. Thus, for example, most people can interpret facial expressions and body language correctly and can understand, to a certain degree, what is implied by the dialogue in texts.

So even if Le Bon might have been mistaken about the degree to which everyone in a crowd or, in modern terms, an audience interprets a text identically, he was correct about the power of these texts to shape people's (or some people's) perceptions and, in many cases, their behavior. If this were not the case, companies would not spend tens and hundreds of millions of dollars on advertising. It makes sense to assume that there are large areas of commonality that people experience in the mass-mediated texts to which they are exposed, even if there are large areas of differences in the way they interpret them and are affected by them.

38 ▷ Television and Art

Commercial television has failed to develop into a new form of meaning-ful communication. It communicates almost nothing that is worth being communicated. Television has failed to utilize a unique opportunity in history. It did not become a new form of art or information. Instead it sold out to the hucksters. It is as if printing had been invented not in order to print the Bible and the works of great literature, but to print handbills, in order to advertise things we do not need and do not want.

Television shows can be analyzed by the methods developed in the analysis of dreams and symbols. A differentiation should be made between the manifest show, which is witnessed by the viewer, and its latent content, which is hidden in the symbolic meaning of the performance and which is beamed simultaneously at our conscious perception and unconscious understanding. Television is analogous to a dream, which has a manifest content and a latent meaning. A television show is a kind of collective dream, which we all dream simultaneously and which can be analyzed as a collective dream. . . .

The intent of contemporary commercial television is different from the intent of the artist. The reaction of the viewer to the television show is therefore also different from an art experience which aims at working through of unconscious conflict. When we view Sophocles' *Oedipus Rex,* Shakespeare's *Hamlet,* or *King Lear,* we perform with our participation another part in the never completed assignment of facing our repressed, unconscious Oedipus complex. In most television shows the intent is to replace tension with attention. . . . Television has utterly failed to become a new form of art experience. Television viewing is not difficult work, but it is a "show," an entertainment; it aims to distract from conflicts and not to solve them.

— Martin Grotjahn, *The Voice of the Symbol* (New York: Delta Books, 1971), 3, 4

Questions for Discussion and Further Research

1. What attacks does Grotjahn make on commercial television? How does advertising fit in here?
2. How does he distinguish between the "manifest" show and the "latent content" of the show?
3. What does he say about the difference between "art" and "television"? Do you agree? Explain.
4. What role does Grotjahn give "entertainment" in our lives?
5. In what ways are television programs like dreams?

According to psychiatrist Martin Grotjahn, television failed to become the artistic and educational medium it could have become and, instead, became one more means of exposing audiences to commercials. Grotjahn laments that television didn't achieve its potential, as a medium, to spread the arts and information of use to citizens. Instead, "it sold out to hucksters." We have to realize that the airwaves belong to the public and that the television networks and local television stations that are allowed to broadcast do so, in theory, in the public's interest.

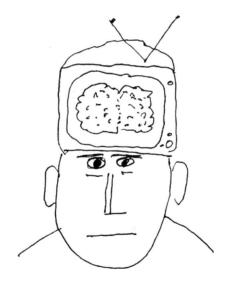

Grotjahn suggests that television can be analyzed the same way dreams are analyzed, in terms of their manifest content, which is what viewers see and hear, and their latent content, which involves the hidden symbolic meaning that registers both on our minds and on unconscious elements in our psyches. He contrasts art and television as follows:

Art	Television
Works through unconscious conflicts	Distracts from conflicts
Tensions about psychic phenomena	Attention to commercials
Participates in facing the repressed	Presents a show that amuses

Grotjahn would no doubt agree that there are some excellent television programs that are broadcast from time to time, but from his perspective, these programs are accidents. Not only has television not lived up to its potential; the implication of Grotjahn's argument is that television is actually harming its audiences by helping them avoid coming to terms with unconscious tensions and other such phenomena in their lives. If television in America is a collective daydream, what do these daydreams reveal about the psyches of the American public that dreams/watches them? And what is television doing to our children? Grotjahn points out that one-sixth of the waking time of most children is devoted to watching television. (Were he writing now, in the twenty-first century, he would have to add something about video games, computers, cell phones, and digital music players, which now are competing with television for the attention of people.)

A Kaiser Foundation media usage study in 2005 provided data of interest relative to the usage of specific media by young people:

3:04 hours a day watching TV
0:14 hours a day watching prerecorded TV
0:32 hours a day watching videos, DVDs
1:44 hours a day listening to music
1:02 hours a day using a computer
0:49 hours a day playing video games
0:43 hours a day reading
0:25 hours a day watching movies

The study also provides information on new media and eight- to eighteen-year-olds, relative to what devices they own and what they do with them:

64% have downloaded music from the Internet
48% have streamed a radio station through the Internet
66% use instant messaging
39% have a cell phone
34% have a DVR such as a TiVo in their homes
35% have created a personal website or web page
18% have an MP3 player
13% have a handheld device that connects to the Internet

39 Amusing Ourselves to Death

Television has become ... the background radiation of the social and intellectual universe, the all-but-imperceptible residue of the electronic big bang of a century past, so familiar and so thoroughly integrated with American culture that we no longer hear its faint hissing in the background or see the flickering gray light. This, in turn, means that its epistemology goes largely unnoticed. And the peek-a-boo world it has constructed around us no longer seems even strange.

There is no more disturbing consequence of the electronic and graphic revolution than this: that the world as given to us through television seems natural, not bizarre. For the loss of the sense of the strange is a sign of adjustment, and the extent to which we have adjusted is a measure of the extent to which we have been changed. Our culture's adjustment to the epistemology of television is by now all but complete; we have so thoroughly accepted its definitions of truth, knowledge, and reality that irrelevance seems to us to be filled with import, and incoherence seems eminently sane. . . .

It is my object in the rest of this book to make the epistemology of television visible again. I will try to demonstrate by concrete example ... that television's conversations promote incoherence and triviality ... and that television speaks in only one persistent voice, the voice of entertainment. Beyond that, I will try to demonstrate that to enter the great television conversation, one American cultural institution after another is learning to speak its terms. Television, in other words, is transforming our culture into one vast arena for show business. It is entirely possible, of course, that in the end we shall find that delightful, and decide we like it just fine. That is exactly what Aldous Huxley feared was coming, fifty years ago.

— Neil Postman, *Amusing Ourselves to Death* (New York: Penguin, 1985), 79–80

Questions for Discussion and Further Research

1. What is it about television that disturbs Postman so much?
2. How does Postman use the term "epistemology"?
3. What does Postman say about the impact of television on American culture?
4. Compare and contrast Grotjahn and Postman on television and society.
5. How can one be "entertained to death"? Explain your answer.

Neil Postman's essay points out how dangerous television is because, as he explains, it seems so natural and part of the scheme of things. As a result of television, he suggests, we have lost our sense of the strangeness of the world and have become adjusted to the "epistemology" of television—to its imperatives and requirements. And it is Postman's self-appointed task to explain this "epistemology." That is, he will deal with the role television plays in making us see the world the way television presents it to us. This televised world, he adds, is full of triviality and incoherence and is based solely on one thing—entertaining us.

The problem, Postman argues, is that television is entertaining us to death. Television, he asserts, has shoved other aspects of life aside and is transforming (and not for the better) American culture and society. Our lives, thanks to television—and its endless commercials, which both entertain and instruct us on what goods and services to buy—are now dominated by a need to be amused and entertained in every aspect of our lives. Shopping, I should add, has now become an entertainment as well. It is an expression of the logic of television, which amuses us and sells us its view of the world and an endless array of products. In a sense, shopping is the actualization of the television commercials to which we are endlessly exposed.

It seems, Postman laments, that America is becoming very much like show business, and what is worse, Americans seem to like it that way. It is, then, a kind of electronic drug. And Postman wants to pull the plug on it, or, at the very least, show what television is doing to American society. Television is the medium everyone loves to hate. Many social scientists have warned us about television, but that hasn't had much impact on the amount of viewing in the United States, where the average person watches more than four hours of television each day. (These often-cited figures come from the A. C. Nielsen Company.) It may be that relatively few people actually "love" television but just about everyone watches it.

Amusing Ourselves to Death

40 ▶ Narratives in the Media

Narrated reality constantly tells us what must be believed and what must be done. What can you oppose to the facts? You can only give in and obey what they "signify," like an oracle of Delphi. The fabrication of simulacra thus provides the means of producing believers and hence people practicing their faiths. . . . This institution of the real no longer has its proper place, neither seat nor *ex cathedra* authority. An anonymous code, information innervates and saturates the body politic. From morning to night, narrations constantly haunt streets and buildings. They articulate our existences by teaching us what they must be. They "cover the event," that is to say, they make our legends (*legenda,* what is to be read and said) out of it.

Captured by the radio (the voice is the law) as soon as he awakens, the listener walks all day long through the forest of narrativities from journalism, advertising, and television narrativities that still find time, as he is getting ready for bed, to slip a few final messages under the portals of sleep. Even more than the God told about by the theologians of earlier days, these stories have a providential and predestining function: they organize in advance our work, our celebrations, and even our dreams. Social life multiplies the gestures and modes of behavior *(im)printed* by narrative models; it ceasely [sic] reproduces and accumulates "copies" of stories. Our society has become a recited society, in three senses: it is defined by *stories* (*recits,* the fables constituted by our advertising and informational media), by *citations* of stories, and by the interminable *recitation* of stories. These narrations have the twofold and strange power of transforming seeing into believing, and of fabricating realities out of appearances.

— Michel de Certeau, *The Practice of Everyday Life* (Berkeley:
  University of California Press, 1984), 186

Questions for Discussion and Further Research

1. What does de Certeau mean by "narrated realities"?
2. Define "narrative" and discuss its role in our everyday lives as de Certeau explains things.
3. What are "genres," and what role do they play in our television viewing?
4. How do narratives affect people, according to de Certeau?
5. In what way is our society a "recited" society? Explain de Certeau's views on this matter.

Michel de Certeau, a prominent French social scientist, offers an important insight into an important aspect of the media. The content of the media is for the most part narratives, which engage us from the moment we get up in the morning until we go to bed at night. (And when we dream, let me add, we dream in narratives that have a number of functions for us.) Narratives—that is, stories—pervade journalism, advertising, television, and all the media. And that is because, as a number of the scholars I've cited in this book point out, we essentially make sense of the world and relate to others, in our conversations, by narratives. Even the national news on television can be considered a narrative, made up of bits and pieces of other smaller narratives—in the form of news reports, also popularly known as "stories," from all over the world.

De Certeau uses the term *imprint* to suggest how the narratives that we see and hear affect us, by providing models for us to imitate, that we don't always do consciously. A school of media analysis known as "uses and gratifications" suggests that people use various kinds of narratives in the media to help them deal with needs they have. For example, a study made years ago found that women listened to soap operas because they believed that these soap operas provided them with insights about how to deal with various problems they faced, as well as providing a certain amount of pleasure from escaping their day-to-day worries. Rather than focusing attention on the effects media have on groups of people, the uses and gratifications scholars look for the way people use the media and examine the gratifications the media offer people. Bruno Bettelheim, in the selection I offer in this book, talks about the all-important role that fairy tales play in the lives of young children, who find that these stories help them deal with unconscious problems they face. In the same light, it is reasonable to assume that the songs adolescents listen to and the television shows and films people watch play a similar role.

The language we use about "watching television" is a form of mystification. People don't watch television—the medium—but watch various programs, most of which are, to varying degrees, narratives. These narratives fall into various genres or kinds of shows: mysteries, science fiction stories, news shows, game shows, reality shows, soap operas, talk shows, sporting events, and so on. What is important to realize about all of these different genres or kinds of programs is that they all have a narrative structure to them, and to the extent that we learn from narratives, all of these genres play a role in shaping our ideas and attitudes that we seldom think about.

41 Television Is a Dramatic Medium

On the most obvious level television is a dramatic medium simply because a large proportion of the material it transmits is in the form of traditional drama mimetically represented by actors and employing plot, dialogue, character, gesture, costume—the whole panoply of dramatic means of expression.... According to the 1980 edition of *The Media Book*, in the Spring of 1979 American men on average watched television for over 21 hours per week, while the average American woman's viewing time reached just over 25 hours per week. The time devoted by the average American adult male to watching dramatic material on television thus amounts to over 12 hours per week, while the average American woman sees almost 16 hours of drama on television each week. That means the average American adult sees the equivalent of *five to six full-length stage plays a week!* ...

Television is the most voyeuristic of all communication media, not only because it provides more material in an unending stream of images and in the form most universally acceptable to the total population, but also because it is the most intimate of the dramatic media. In the theater, the actors are relatively remote from the audience, and the dramatic occasion is public. In the cinema, also a public occasion gathering a large audience into a single room, the actors are nearer to the spectators than in the theater, but in close-ups they are larger than life. Television is seen at close range and in a more private context. The close-up of the television performer is on a scale that most nearly approximates direct human contact.

— Martin Esslin, *The Age of Television* (San Francisco: W. H. Freeman, 1982), 7, 30, 32

Questions for Discussion and Further Research

1. What are the "dramatic means of expression," according to Esslin?
2. How does Esslin use the term "voyeuristic"? What impact does this voyeurism have on viewers of TV?
3. What is a "parasocial" relationship? How does this affect television viewers?
4. What arguments does Esslin offer about the impact of televised narratives on viewers and society?

The statistics on television viewing in the United States are quite incredible. It is estimated by the A. C. Nielsen Company that the average person in America watches around four hours of television every day, which means that television viewing is the dominant leisure-time activity for most people. Media scholars have made studies that reveal that the average young person in America spends between six and nine hours per day with one form of media or another: television, video games, music, and so on. Children two to seven spend about three and a half hours with media each day, and children eight and older spend almost seven hours with media each day. (These statistics are cited in the Grotjahn selection and can be found at the Kaiser Family Foundation's website at www.kff.org.)

Esslin points out something rather significant about our television watching: Adult Americans, who watch three or four hours of television each day, "see the equivalent of five to six full-length plays a week." This is the equivalent of going to the theater five or six days a week. It is an important figure when we realize the power that narratives have upon people. Some television viewers tend to think of actors and actresses they watch on television as friends or people they know—this is called having a parasocial relationship. Television is often described as a "close-up medium" that creates the illusion in the minds of some viewers that they are actually *with* other people. That is why some heavy viewers have parasocial relationships with television performers, why they feel (or, more precisely, they have the illusion) that they "know them" intimately. It is not the same thing as a real relationship with someone else and suggests that something is lacking in terms of real social relationships in the lives of people with these parasocial relationships.

Consider the content of most of the narratives to which we are exposed when we watch television—they are full of violence and sexual innuendo (verging, in some cases, on pornography) and are interrupted endlessly by commercials—which themselves are micronarratives. There is reason to be alarmed about what these five or six full-length plays are doing to us, as adults, and what they are doing to our children. Martin Grotjahn, in his selection, castigated television as a medium that sold out to hucksters and gave up on becoming a medium that would enhance our well-being, help us become more refined, and educate us, in the broadest sense of the term. Martin Esslin points out the way television works—it is a medium dominated by narratives that have the power to shape our behavior and our desires and is used by corporations selling products and services to do so. This is a further elaboration on the argument made by Michel de Certeau about the role narratives play in people's lives.

In the selection that follows, on rock music, we turn our attention to the role of music in the lives of adolescents and others. Songs are also narratives that are sung to us by vocalists in rock bands and other kinds of bands. Songs have the power they do because of their components: a beat, rhythm, rhyme, melody, and the human voice.

42   The Power of Rock Music

Rock must be understood ... as a form of music. Its cultural effects have musical causes. One difficulty here is that rock is a song form—there is a temptation to analyze the words at the expense of the sounds. Words can be reproduced for comment with comparative ease, and rhymes are better understood than chords; sociologists of popular music have always fallen for the easy terms of lyrical analysis. Such a word-based approach is not helpful at getting at the meaning of rock. The fans know, in Greil Marcus's words, that "words are sounds we can feel before they are statements to understand." Most rock records make their impact musically rather than lyrically. The words, if they are noticed at all, are absorbed after the music has made its mark. The crucial variables are sound and music....

Rock's cultural significance is as a form of music. ... Rock is made *in order* to have emotional, social, physical, commercial results; it is not music made "for its own sake." As Lester Bangs puts his doubts about Blondie's avant-garde "serious" pretensions,

> If the main reason we listen to music in the first place is to hear passion expressed—as I've believed all my life—then what *good* is this music going to prove to be? (Lester Bangs, *Blondie* [New York: Fireside, 1980], 70)

—Simon Frith, *Sound Effects: Youth, Leisure, and the Politics of Rock 'n' Roll* (New York: Pantheon, 1981), 14–15

Questions for Discussion and Further Research

1. What does Frith say about the relation between words and sound in rock?
2. Frith says sociologists tend to make mistakes when analyzing rock. What are they?
3. What does Bangs say about music and passion in rock? Can Bangs's ideas be applied to all music?
4. Frith says rock's social effects are based on the voice. What does that mean?
5. Investigate how the human voice affects people and explain what you've found.

Rock is, in a sense, primitive. It uses a primitive understanding of how sounds and rhythms—prelinguistic devices—have their emotional and physical effects. Its sound effects are those of daily life. The sound questions raised are nonmusical: Why do we respond the way we do to a baby's cry, a stranger's laugh, a loud, steady beat? Because so much of rock music depends on the social effects of the voice, the questions about how rock's effects are produced are vocal, not musical. What makes a voice haunting? sexy? chilling?

One mistake many critics of rock make, Frith argues, is to focus attention only on the words in songs and neglect the music. If you look at the lyrics of some rock songs, they seem quite simple minded and trite. But when you add the music, the situation changes—for it is the music and the emotion generated by the music that is of paramount importance. Rock may make "primitive" use of sounds and rhythms, but the impact of rock music can be very powerful.

If you think about the rock concerts held in football stadiums and in other similar venues, you sense that something rather significant is going on. There is now a gigantic audience for rock music, and many longtime rock groups such as the Rolling Stones, full of somewhat long in the tooth stars, still continue to perform. The lighting, the power of the amplification, the rituals in some of these rock concerts all suggest something very close to the sacred. Barthes pointed out in *Mythologies* (1972) that light without shadow generates "an emotion without reserve," which may explain, in part, why these concerts have the power they do.

The main reason we listen to music, Frith says, is to experience emotions, to feel the passion in the music and in the voices of rock singers. This may explain why music plays such an important role in the lives of young people. They are all experiencing powerful and often conflicting emotions, and the music they listen to somehow speaks to them and helps them deal with their difficulties, much the way fairy tales do for children. Frith ends this passage with a question—how do you explain the power of the human voice, and what is it that makes a voice "haunting," "sexy," or "chilling"?

We could ask the same thing about voices in other kinds of music such as opera or country western. But I would suggest it isn't only the quality of a singer's voice that is important; the lyrics of songs and their melodies also play important roles.

43 ▶ Artistic Texts

Art is a special means of communication, a language organized in a particular manner (our concept of language derives from the broad semiotic definition: any ordered system which serves as a means of communication and employs signs), the works of art, that is, messages in this language, can be viewed as texts. . . .

The tendency to interpret *everything* in an artistic text as meaningful is so great that we rightfully consider nothing accidental in a work of art. . . . Art is the most economical, compact method for storing and transmitting information. But art has other properties wholly worthy of the attention of cyberneticians and perhaps, in time, design engineers. Since it can concentrate a tremendous amount of information into the "area" of a very small text (cf. The length of a short story by Cexov [Chekov] and a psychology textbook) an artistic text manifests yet another feature: it transmits different information to different readers in proportion to each one's comprehension; it provides the reader with a language in which each successive portion of information may be assimilated with repeated reading. It behaves as a kind of living organism which has a feedback channel to the reader and thereby instructs him.

— Yuri Lotman, *The Structure of the Artistic Text* (Ann Arbor: Michigan Slavic Contributions, 1977), 6, 17, 23

Questions for Discussion and Further Research

1. How does Lotman define art? What specific properties does he say art has?
2. What does it mean to say that art is a language?
3. How does he explain our pleasure in reading the same text over and over again?
4. Apply Lotman's theory about art to rock music. Does it work? Justify your position.
5. Do Lotman's ideas apply to pop culture as well as serious art? Explain why or why not.
6. Why do some rock songs last while most of them fade into oblivion? What would Lotman say?

Yuri Lotman is associated with the Tartu (Russia) school of semiotics and has written on the semiotics of film and other aspects of culture. This selection offers us an explanation of why we can derive pleasure from seeing a film several times or reading a novel several times or listening to music over and over again. Lotman's point is that works of art are very complicated and "dense," and that when people see a film or read a novel, the first time, they take (maybe "skim off" is a better term) some information from the text. But they don't extract all the information in the text, because of its richness and complexity. So each time we see a film or experience any kind of work of art, we get more out of it—and the process is endless.

In addition, this quality is special to works of art. Lotman explains that "literature possesses an exclusive, inherent system of signs and rules governing their combination which serve to transmit special messages, nontransmittable by other means" (1977, 21). We can extend this notion of literature to all the arts, I would suggest. Works of art have incredible richness, density, and power, which explains why people find art such a necessary part of their lives.

Critics like Martin Esslin and Fredric Jameson argue that the popular arts, however, are much "weaker" kinds of art and don't help people deal with unconscious problems and gain an understanding of what it is to be human but, instead, pander to people's basest instincts and are escapist in nature. Whether this is true is subject to debate. One thing is certain: The greatest works of art and literature (and the so-called elite arts) continue to be meaningful to people over hundreds, and in some cases, thousands of years, while most of the texts found in contemporary popular culture tend to be discarded after a very short period of time.

44 Psychoanalysis and Literature

The supreme virtue of psychoanalysis, from the point of view of its potential utility for literary study, is that it has investigated the very aspects of man's nature with which the greatest writers of fiction have been preoccupied: the emotional unconscious or only partly comprehended bases of our behavior. Unlike other psychologies, but like Sophocles and Shakespeare, Tolstoy and Dostoevsky, Melville and Hawthorne, it has concerned itself with the surging non-rational forces which play so large a part in determining our destiny as well as the part of our being which tries, often in vain, to control and direct them. It offers a systematic and well-validated body of knowledge about those forces.

It ought to be apparent that the finding of such a psychology should be helpful in explicating many of the things conveyed through fiction—and in particular the deepest levels of meaning of the greatest fiction. I deliberately use the word *explicate*. It is my assumption that as we read we unconsciously *understand* at least some of a story's secret significance; to some extent our enjoyment is a product of this understanding. But some readers go on to try to account for the effect a story has had upon them, and to report what they discover. It is in connection with these later critical activities, which must be differentiated I believe from the reading experience itself, that psychoanalytic concepts are likely to prove invaluable. They make it possible to deal with a portion of our response which was not hitherto accessible to criticism—permit us to explain reactions which were intuitive, fugitive and often non-verbal, and supply the key to the elements in the story responsible for those reactions.

— Simon O. Lesser, *Fiction and the Unconscious* (Boston: Beacon Press, 1957), 15

Questions for Discussion and Further Research

1. How does psychoanalytic theory help literary study, according to Lesser? Be explicit.
2. What assumptions does Lesser make about what happens when we read (or watch films, see TV shows)?
3. How does psychoanalytic theory help us bring to light the "hidden meanings" in texts?
4. What does Lesser say about how the arts help us deal with psychic conflicts?
5. Find an article that offers a psychoanalytic interpretation of a specific text and report on it in class.

Simon Lesser is writing about fiction in this selection, but his insights can be applied to all art forms and texts in all media. We have to recognize that analysts and critics of the media, and the texts they carry, always come to their subject with certain notions and ideas of what is most important in interpreting texts. Criticism is always tied to the ideology or discipline or beliefs of the critic, which explains why there are psychoanalytic critics, Marxist critics, ethical critics, semiotic critics, feminist critics, and so on. Some critics combine several points of view, so one might find psychoanalytic feminist critics or Marxist semiotic critics and all kinds of other combinations of disciplines and perspectives on texts in all media.

What Lesser suggests is that psychoanalytic criticism, which focuses on the human psyche, the unconscious, and various drives and defense mechanisms we use to keep our balance, has a particularly useful role to play, for it explains the "secret significance" of stories and other texts and helps us understand why works of art speak to us the way they do. Why do we react the way we do to certain films, novels, television shows, and other texts? Why is it that at the end of some plays and movies and novels we find ourselves profoundly moved, sometimes to tears? In some cases these works can even change our lives.

Lesser argues that we get pleasure from understanding, to the extent we do, the hidden meanings in these texts. There is, one might suggest, a communication from the unconscious of the artists and creators of texts to the unconscious of the readers and viewers of these texts. And texts, as Lotman has pointed out, are very complex and deep, and so we get different things out of them each time we experience them.

The arts (of all kinds), Lesser claims, help us deal with the fact that at every stage of our lives we are unsatisfied and the pleasures we get from life are transitory. The arts help us gain a measure of pleasure and joy by providing us with a more harmonious world, a different world, a bounded world, one that contrasts with our own lives that just go on and on, whose beginnings are more or less lost to us in the distant past and whose ends we try to put off as long as we can. Technically speaking, from a psychoanalytic perspective, works of art help us deal with the ongoing conflict between our ids and superegos, between our desire for pleasure and our feelings of guilt. As Freud put it, explaining the role of the superego in helping curb our aggressive impulses, "Civilization, therefore, obtains mastery of the individual's dangerous desire for aggression by weakening it and dismantling it and by setting up an agency within him to watch over it, like a garrison in a conquered city" (1962, 71).

45 Humor and Communication

Humor is seen as play—an interpersonal process or communication which either starts out contained in a play frame or which is suddenly caught into such a frame from behind when the episode is at the point of termination. The play frame indicates that the process is unreal; the process is on a different level of abstraction from the laugh that follows it. . . . The punch line is protean; it may be expressed in any one of the ways by which humans communicate. It may be words—or other sounds; it may be movement or gesture, an expression, a situation. There are no rules about what punch lines have to be. But punch lines are essential. . . . A joke (of any variety) is play with a climax. . . . Apparently it is just as essential that humor have this climax as it is for humor to be surrounded by a play frame.

During the unfolding of humor, one is suddenly confronted by an explicit-implicit reversal when the punch line is delivered. The reversal helps distinguish humor from play, dreams, etc. Sudden reversals such as characterize the punch line moment in humor are disruptive and foreign to play. . . . The reversal also has the unique effect of forcing upon the humor participants an internal redefining of reality. Inescapably, the punch line combines communication and metacommunication. One receives the explicit communication of the punch line. Also, on a higher level of abstraction, the punch line carries an implicit metacommunication about itself and about reality as exemplified by the joke.

— William F. Fry Jr., *Sweet Madness: A Study of Humor* (Palo Alto, CA: Pacific Books, 1963), 146, 153

Questions for Discussion and Further Research

1. What does Fry mean by "play frames," and what role do they have in humor?
2. What does Fry say about different kinds of punch lines?
3. What is "metacommunication"? What role does Fry say it plays in humor?
4. How does humor "trick" the superego? Why does this give us pleasure?
5. Explain the incongruity, masked aggression, and superiority theories of humor.
6. Use the forty-five techniques of humor to reveal the techniques at work in some jokes.

William Fry is a Stanford psychiatrist who has done important work on all aspects of humor. He has studied the biological effects of humor; he has tickled chimps to see whether it can be determined that they have a sense of humor. And he has written on the complexities of humor as a form of communication. In his book *Sweet Madness* he deals with the fact that humor usually involves some kind of a "frame" that informs people who go to see comedians that the comedian doesn't really mean it when he insults people of all kinds, says all kinds of nasty things about husbands, wives, children, politicians, and so on. Humor differs from play in that humor—especially in the form of humor known as the joke—has a punch line. Jokes can be defined as short stories, meant to amuse, that have punch lines. Usually this punch line comes as a big surprise and makes us interpret what we had been told in a joke up to the punch line in a different manner.

Fry uses the term *metacommunication*, which means, in short, communication about communication. Thus, when we watch a comedian (or go see a comedy) we have the expectation from experiences with other comedians that they don't really mean what they say. Otherwise, the aggressive nature of their jokes and monologues would distress listeners. Freud argued that humor involves masked or hidden aggression. The humor prevents our superegos from taking what is said seriously. Other analysts have argued that humor is based on incongruities—on the difference between what we expect and what we get. A punch line, from this perspective, is an example of an incongruity.

Some theorists, such as Aristotle and Hobbes, argue that humor is based on a sense of superiority, and we laugh at people who have been made (or who make themselves) ridiculous. Hobbes is famous for writing in *The Leviathan*, "The passion of laughter is nothing else but sudden glory arising from a sudden conception of some eminence in ourselves by comparison with the infirmities of others, or with our own formerly." Fry belongs to a fourth group of humor scholars who see humor as tied to complexities of communication and to the use of play frames and paradoxes as basic to the creation and appreciation of humor. All of these theories attempt to explain why we laugh.

My own work on humor has involved focusing my attention on what makes people laugh rather than why people laugh. As the result of a content analysis I made of humorous texts of all kinds, I elicited forty-five techniques that I suggest are the building blocks of humor. I explain these techniques and show how humorists have used them in An Anatomy of Humor and The Art of Comedy Writing. The chart below lists my forty-five techniques:

Techniques of Humor in Alphabetical Order

1. Absurdity	16. Embarrassment	31. Parody
2. Accident	17. Exaggeration	32. Puns
3. Allusion	18. Exposure	33. Repartee
4. Analogy	19. Facetiousness	34. Repetition
5. Before/After	20. Grotesque	35. Reversal
6. Bombast	21. Ignorance	36. Ridicule
7. Burlesque	22. Imitation	37. Rigidity
8. Caricature	23. Impersonation	38. Sarcasm
9. Catalogue	24. Infantilism	39. Satire
10. Chase scene	25. Insults	40. Scale, size
11. Coincidence	26. Irony	41. Slapstick
12. Comparison	27. Literalness	42. Speed
13. Definition	28. Mimicry	43. Stereotypes
14. Disappointment	29. Mistakes	44. Theme and variations
15. Eccentricity	30. Misunderstanding	45. Unmasking

This list is somewhat controversial, and some humor scholars have suggested it could be reduced considerably. It is possible, I suggest, to use these techniques to find out what mechanisms are at play in jokes and other forms of humor.

Humor remains a subject about which there is much interest in academic circles, and it has been studied by philosophers, psychiatrists, psychologists, sociologists, folklorists, and all kinds of other scholars and thinkers for thousands of years. Aristotle is supposed to have written a book on comedy, but it has never been found. And every year, books that offer examples of humor or that claim to teach people how to be funny or that argue about the nature of humor continue to be written. Humor is a means that we have evolved to help us learn about ourselves and our situations and to enhance, if only for a short while, while we laugh, our enjoyment of life.

46 On Comedy

Epic poetry and Tragedy, Comedy also and Dithyrambic poetry and the music of the flute and of the lyre in most of the forms are all in their general conception modes of imitation. They differ, however, from one another in three respects—the medium, the objects, the manner or mode of imitation, being in each case distinct.

For as there are persons who, by conscious art or mere habit, imitate and represent various objects through the medium of colour and form, or again by the voice; so in the arts above mentioned, taken as a whole, the imitation is produced by rhythm, language, or "harmony," either singly or combined.

Since the objects of imitation are men of action, and these must be either of a higher or a lower type (for moral character mainly answers to these divisions, goodness and badness being the distinguishing marks of moral differences), it follows that we must represent men either as better than in real life, or as worse, or as they are. . . . Comedy aims at representing men as worse, Tragedy as better than in actual life. . . .

Comedy is, as we have said, an imitation of characters of a lower type—not, however, in the full sense of the word bad, the Ludicrous being merely a subdivision of the ugly. It consists of some defect which is not painful or destructive. . . . Tragedy, then, is an imitation of an action that is serious, and of a certain magnitude; in language embellished with each kind of artistic ornament, the several kinds being found in separate parts of the play; in the form of action, not of narrative; through pity and fear effecting the proper purgation of these emotions.

— Aristotle, "Poetics," in *The Great Critics: An Anthology of Literary Criticism,* 3rd ed., ed. James Harry Smith and Edd Winfield Parks (New York: W. W. Norton, 1951), 28–34

Questions for Discussion and Further Research

1. Explain Aristotle's theory that art is based on imitation.
2. How does comedy fit into Aristotle's theory of art? Does that explain why sitcoms are so popular?
3. What other theories of art are there? Explain how they work.
4. What are the arguments in the debate on media violence? How do you feel? Justify your position.
5. What's the difference between tragedy and comedy? Between cathexis and catharsis?
6. How does Girard's theory of "mimetic desire" explain how advertising works?

Aristotle (384 to 322 BC) is one of the most influential philosophers, who wrote on many different subjects (ethics, politics, rhetoric) and whose ideas dominated our thinking for centuries. According to Aristotle, art should be seen as an imitation of life—a theory known as the mimetic theory of art. There are four dominant theories of art:

Pragmatic: Art is used to do something, accomplish some goal.
Objective: Art projects a reality as seen by the artist.
Emotive: Art gives us kicks and generates emotional responses.
Mimetic: Art imitates reality.

What art imitates, Aristotle says, is "men in action," and these men are either "high" types, whose actions we follow in tragedies, or "low" types, whose actions we follow in comedies. As the result of attending tragedies, people experience pity and fear, which leads to a purgation of their emotions. Aristotle's "Poetics" offers what is probably the first elaboration of the mimetic theory of art, but it also makes room for the emotive theory.

There is a big debate among media scholars about the effects of televised violence on audiences. Some scholars argue that televised

aristotle

violence leads to antisocial behavior in their viewers, who imitate, in various ways, the violence they have seen on television. Others argue that televised violence purges viewers of hostile feelings and thus does not lead to viewers acting out and being violent. This theory is known as the catharsis theory. Research evidence suggests that exposure to violent television programs (and one might add films and videos, as well) does lead to increased violent behavior, though it sometimes takes years for this violent behavior to manifest itself, and not everyone who is exposed to violence is affected by it.

Martin Esslin and others argue that television shows don't, as a rule, lead to the kind of purgation we get from seeing a great work of art, such as *King Lear*, but prevent us from having powerful emotional experiences and distract us from the task of resolving our inner conflicts. It can be suggested, then, that Aristotle's ideas about purgation from works of art might be correct if we were exposed to serious works of art, works that, as Aristotle put it, have a certain "magnitude."

At the end of a serious work of tragedy, the stage is generally littered with dead bodies. Think, for example, of *Hamlet*. There is a kind of inevitability to Hamlet's death and a high seriousness that pervades the play. At the end of a work of comedy, there is usually a celebration and a wedding and a feeling of optimism and freedom. We can see the relationship between tragedies and comedies in the chart that follows, which draws upon other aspects of tragedy and comedy by various theorists:

Tragedy	*Comedy*
Men higher than ordinary	Men lower than ordinary
High status	Low status
Determinism	Freedom
High seriousness	Not serious at all
Pessimism	Optimism
Pain	Pleasure
Catharsis	Cathexis

The world of comedy is the world of chance, of coincidences, of mistakes and misunderstandings, but as we know, from the fact that we are seeing a comedy, everything will turn out for the best, and generally speaking, lovers who have been kept separated by one thing or another finally get together, and generally get married. There is a cathexis, a release of pent-up energy that is life affirming and celebratory, as contrasted to a catharsis in tragedy, where we experience profound emotions at the tragic fate of the heroes and heroines in these plays.

A French literary scholar, Rene Girard, uses the concept of mimesis to help explain advertising. In his book *A Theatre of Envy: William Shakespeare*, he argues that "mimetic desire" is at work in advertising—we imitate the desire of the stars and celebrities we see in advertisements and commercials. He believes that "mimetic desire" also can be used to interpret Shakespeare's plays and much behavior in people. Thus he explains Helen of Troy and the Trojan War as follows: "The only reason the Greeks want her back is because the Trojans want to keep her. The only reason the Trojans want to keep her is because the Greeks want her back" (1991, 123). If Girard is correct, "mimetic desire" is a force that explains a great deal of human behavior—and it stems, of course, from Aristotle's theory of art as mimesis. Art imitates life, says Aristotle, and life imitates art, adds Girard.

47 ▶ What Does Art Do?

F EW questions can have been debated so long as "What is Art?" to so little purpose; it is time this nonsense ceased. For in fact the question is unanswerable in this form; it is in the same category as Electricity, Light, or Instinct. And just as you can answer "What is Instinct?" only with something like "Instinct is what makes birds fly south in Fall," so you can define Art only in terms of function.

Instead of asking "What is Art?" we need to ask "What kinds of things have been done by that activity traditionally called Art?" And then we will find that activity historically performed four functions: substitute imagery; illustration; conviction and persuasion; and beautification. (1) In cases where the appearance of something needed to be preserved for one reason or another, art made pictures that could be substituted for the actual thing. (2) Art made images or shapes (including pictographs) that could be used in whole or part to tell stories or record events vividly ("illustrate," "illuminate," "elucidate," all come from the same root "lux" = "light"). (3) Art made images which by association of shapes with ideas set forth the fundamental convictions or realized ideals of societies (usually in what we call architectural or sculptural form); or conversely art made images intended to persuade people to new or different beliefs (usually in more ephemeral media). (4) Art beautified the world by pleasing the eye or gratifying the mind; what particular combinations of forms, arrangements, colors, proportions or ornament accomplished this end in any given society depended, of course, on what kinds of illustration or conviction or persuasion a given society required its arts to provide.

— Alan Gowans, *The Unchanging Arts: New Forms for the Traditional Functions of Art in Society* (Philadelphia: J. B. Lippincott, 1971), 12–13

Questions for Discussion and Further Research

1. Explain the four functions of art that Gowans deals with.
2. Does Gowans explain what art is?
3. Compare and contrast the four functions of art with the four theories of art.
4. Apply Gowans's theory to the mass media. Which functions dominate our media? Explain why.
5. How can an artist "create reality"? What would Aristotle say? Why?

Gowans cuts through the Gordian knot that is art (and by this I mean all the arts) by asking not what art is but what its functions have been over the years. We may never be able to decide what art is—and some critics have suggested that art has become whatever you want it to be, or anything you can get away with. The way to understand art is to examine its functions over the ages and not quibble about whether art is imitation, as Aristotle suggests, or anything else. We can answer the question of what art does by looking at how it has been used. If we do this we find that art has had four functions over the ages:

1. *Substitute imagery:* works such as photos, paintings, and so on that capture reality
2. *Illustration:* works that tell stories or help tell stories
3. *Conviction and persuasion:* works that show beliefs, sell products
4. *Beautification:* works that please the eye or gratify the mind

It is these four functions that help us understand art, and, Gowans suggests, these are the only important functions of art. That is why Gowans titles his book *The Unchanging Arts*. While different styles of painting may come and go, from abstract expressionism to pop art, the functions of painting haven't changed. And the same applies to other kinds of arts as well.

In some cases, a work of art may have several functions. Consider, for example, video games. The development of digital technology has made it possible to create remarkable texts that are incredibly immersive and, in many cases, addictive. In terms of their function as works of art, we could say that illustration is the dominant function of video games—in that they tell or help tell stories, but they also can involve conviction and beautification.

It is possible to compare Gowans's functions with the typology on the four kinds of art and find some interesting similarities without doing too much violence to facts and stretching things too much:

Functions of Art	Theories of Art
Substitute imagery	Mimetic
Illustration	Objective
Persuasion	Pragmatic
Beautification	Emotive

I don't want to push these comparisons too far, but it is evident that persuasion is similar to the pragmatic theory of art, and a case can be made that beautification and the emotive theory of art are similar, as well. The mimetic theory, which suggests that art imitates reality, is close to the notion that art creates substitute imagery. The objective theory, which states that art creates a reality rather than imitating one, is also similar to Gowans's notion of illustration reflecting the fundamental convictions of society. Philosophers have speculated about the nature of art for thousands of years. One thing Gowans does is enable us to bypass questions about what art is by focusing our attention on what art does.

48 Interpretation and Art

What the overemphasis on the idea of content entails is the perennial, never consummated project of *interpretation*. And conversely, it is the habit of approaching works of art in order to *interpret* them that sustains the fancy that there really is such a thing as the content of a work of art.

Of course I don't mean interpretation in the broadest sense, the sense in which Nietzsche (rightly) says "There are no facts, only interpretations." By interpretation, I mean here a conscious act of the mind which illustrates a certain code, certain "rules" of interpretation. . . . The old style of interpretation was insistent, but respectful; it erected another meaning on top of the literal one. The modern style of interpretation excavates, and as it excavates, destroys; it digs "behind" the text, to find a sub-text which is the true one. The most celebrated and influential modern doctrines, those of Marx and Freud, actually amount to . . . aggressive and imperious theories of interpretation. All observable phenomena are bracketed, in Freud's phrase, as *manifest content*. This manifest content must be probed and pushed aside to find the true meaning—the *latent content*—beneath. For Marx, social events like revolutions and wars; for Freud, the events of individual lives (like neurotic symptoms and slips of the tongue) as well as texts (like a dream or a work of art)—are all treated as occasions for interpretation. According to Marx and Freud, these events only *seem* to be intelligible. Actually, they have no meaning without interpretation. To understand is to interpret. And to interpret is to restate the phenomenon, in effect to find an equivalent for it. . . . Interpretation is the revenge of the intellect upon art.

Even more. It is the revenge of the intellect upon the world.

— Susan Sontag, *Against Interpretation* (New York: Laurel Books, 1970), 15–17

Questions for Discussion and Further Research

1. How does Sontag compare the "old style" and "new style" of interpretation?
2. What does she say about Marxist and Freudian modes of interpretation?
3. Why does she argue that interpretation is the revenge of the intellect on art and on the world?
4. Can we be exposed to a text without interpreting it? Justify your answer.
5. What would various theorists I've dealt with in this book say about Sontag's argument?

Susan Sontag argues that interpretation is "the revenge of intellect upon the world." That may be true, but that is because human beings, so it seems, have intellects and feel it necessary to use them whenever possible. And human beings have erected grandiose theories that explain all kinds of different phenomena, including works of art, from a variety of perspectives. Sontag mentions two—the psychoanalytic and the Marxist perspective. The Freudian psychoanalytic perspective argues that texts have manifest and latent contents; the manifest content is what happens in the story, and the latent content is what the events of the story mean and how they relate to the reader's psyche and unconscious.

The Marxist perspective ties works of art to political and ideological considerations, arguing that these works have to be understood as instruments of manipulation or hegemonic ideological domination by the ruling class, which has a stake in spreading "false consciousness" in the masses.

One might also add that creative artists also are intellectuals and that they spend a great deal of time analyzing and interpreting works by others in an attempt to find a voice and style. That explains why film schools teach courses in film history and art students study art history. Creation doesn't occur in a mindless state, in a void, where neither intellect nor social forces are of any importance. It is also true that in many cases, the best interpreters and critics of the arts are artists, poets, novelists, and so on, themselves. Interpretation may be, as Sontag puts it so eloquently, "the revenge of the intellect upon art" and the world, but the alternative isn't particularly palatable or desirable—unthinking responses to art and the world.

49 ▸ The Society of Spectacle

But certainly for the present age, which prefers the sign to the thing signi-fied, the copy to the original, fancy to reality, the appearance to the essence . . . illusion *only is* sacred, truth *profane. Nay, sacredness is held to be enhanced in proportion as truth decreases and illusion increases, so that the highest degree of illusion comes to be the highest degree of sacredness.* (Feurbach, Preface to the Second Edition of *The Essence of Christianity*)

1. In societies where the modern conditions of production prevail, all of life presents itself as an immense accumulation of *spectacles*. Everything that was directly lived has moved away into a representation.

2. The images detached from every aspect of life fuse into a common stream in which the unity of this life can no longer be reestablished. Reality considered *partially* unfolds, in its own general unity, as a pseudo-world *apart,* an object of mere contemplation. The specialization of images of the world is completed in the world of the autonomous image, where the liar has lied to himself. The spectacle in general, as the concrete inversion of life, is the autonomous movement of the non-living. . . .

3. The spectacle is not a collection of images, but a social relation among people, mediated by images. . . .

4. The spectacle, grasped in its totality, is both the result and the project of the existing mode of production. It is not a supplement to the real world, an additional decoration. It is the heart of the unrealism of the real society. In all its specific forms, as information or propaganda, as advertisement or direct entertainment consumption, the spectacle is the present *model* of socially dominant life. It is the omnipresent affirmation of the choice *already made* in production and its corollary consumption. The spectacle's form and content are identically the total justification of the existing system's conditions and goals. The spectacle is also the *permanent presence* of this justification, since it occupies the main part of the time lived outside of modern production.

— Guy Debord, *Society of the Spectacle* (Michigan: Black & Red, 1967). Quoted in Menashi Gigi Durham and Douglas M. Kellner, eds., *Media and Cultural Studies* (Malden, MA: Blackwell, 2001), 139–140

Questions for Discussion and Further Research

1. What did Feurbach say about illusion and sacredness? Do you agree? Explain your reasons.
2. What did Debord say about spectacle and representation? The role of images?
3. How does Debord tie spectacles to the mode of production in capitalist countries?
4. In what ways do the media justify the status quo? How do images work here?
5. How do spectacles generate "false consciousness"? Why is this important?
6. Can the media ever not generate "false consciousness"? Justify your position.

Guy Debord is a Marxist theorist who focuses his attention on the role of the media, popular culture, and other forms of representation in justifying the status quo. He starts his book by quoting the philosopher Ludwig Feuerbach on the way illusions dominate our thinking, on the notion that we prefer "the sign to the thing signified, the copy to the original, fancy to reality." This leads Debord to analyze the way illusions and representations dominate the thinking of the ordinary person in a series of numbered statements.

He begins his book by arguing that in modern industrialized societies, life is dominated by an endless succession of spectacles, and we've moved from the direct experience of life into a life dominated by representations. This leads him to suggest that images have now become autonomous and dominate our lives, a terrible inversion in which nonliving or unreal aspects of life now are more important than our life experiences. It is important to recognize, he continues, that what he means by "spectacle" is not just a series of images but the social relationships that exist among people that are mediated by these images. The images are a reflection of a more basic matter: the social relationships found in a given society.

And this relationship, he claims, reproducing an argument made by Marx, is tied to the mode of production in societies where spectacles are dominant. His language is a bit difficult to follow in statement 6, but the point is that once the mode of production is determined—as, for example, in capitalism, then the dominance of images and spectacles is assured, for these devices are the means by which the bourgeoisie generates false consciousness in the minds of those who are dominated, the proletariat. The proletariat are the workers, the common people. The spectacles are produced by a group of artists and writers and performers who are servants of the bourgeoisie and constitute what Marxists call the "petite-bourgeoisie," what we would call knowledge workers.

In Marxist thought, the base or mode of production shapes (but does not completely determine) the superstructure—which refers to the institutions in a society that shape the consciousness of its members. Marx argued that the ideas of the ruling classes are always the ideas of the masses, because the ruling classes control the media and thus can shape the consciousness of the masses. Marxist theory is no longer fashionable, especially in the realm of economics. But his ideas about the role of media in shaping people's consciousness still have resonance, especially as the ownership and control of the media are now increasingly centralized, and most of the media are controlled by a small number of people. Debord's ideas have been very influential, and we can trace the ideas of many postmodernist theorists to his focus on images and spectacles in his writings.

Representation and Difference

Q uestions of "difference" have come to the fore in cultural studies in recent years and have been addressed in different ways by different disciplines. In this section we consider four such theoretical accounts. . . .

1. The first account comes from linguistics—from the sort of approach associated with Saussure and the use of language as a model of how culture works. . . . The main argument advanced here is that *"difference" matters because it is essential to meaning: without it nothing could not exist.* We know what *black* means, Saussure argued, not because there is some essence of "blackness" but because we can contrast it with its opposite—*white.*

2. The second explanation comes from theories of language, but from a somewhat different school to that represented by Saussure. *The argument here is that we need "difference" because we can only construct meaning through a dialogue with the "Other."* The great Russian linguist and critic Mikhail Bakhtin . . . studied language, not (as the Saussureans did) as an objective system, but in terms of how meaning is sustained in the *dialogue* between two or more speakers.

3. The third kind of explanation is anthropological. . . . *The argument here is that culture depends on giving things meaning by assigning them to different positions within a classificatory system.* Mary Douglas . . . argues that social groups impose meaning on the world by ordering and organizing things into classificatory systems. Binary oppositions are crucial for all classifications, because one must establish a clear difference between things in order to classify them.

4. The fourth kind of explanation is psychoanalytic and relates to the role of "difference" in our psychic life. *The argument here is that the "Other" is fundamental to the constitution of the self, to us as subjects and to sexual identity.*

— Stuart Hall, "What Does 'Difference' Matter?" in *Representation: Cultural Representations and Signifying Practices,* ed. Stuart Hall (London: Sage Publications, 1997), 234–237

Questions for Discussion and Further Research

1. List and discuss in detail Hall's four different theories about representation.
2. Why is "difference" such an important concept?
3. Which theory of difference seems most compelling to you? Explain your answer.
4. Relate Hall's ideas and theories to selections in this book by various authors.
5. Is there a difference between "difference" and "opposition"? Justify your position.

Stuart Hall, a well-known British media scholar, argues that "difference" is a fundamental aspect of the way we make sense of the world and offers four ways in which theorists have explained "difference." Hall focuses on difference because it is involved with how people find meaning in the world. The four ways he describes are not mutually exclusive, since they focus on the linguistic, the social, the cultural, and the psychic levels, respectively. Hall starts with Saussure, who wrote in his pioneering book *Course in General Linguistics* that "in language there are only differences" (1966, 120). Saussure argued that meaning comes from the relationship that exists between concepts; that is, things don't have essential meanings but relational ones. Black has meaning not because there is some essence of blackness, Hall says, but because we can contrast black with white, and it is the difference between the two that generates meaning.

Another theory of difference stems from the work of the Russian linguist Mikhail Bakhtin, who suggested that meaning stems from dialogue—a theory known as dialogism. In this theory, meaning arises from "the give and take between different speakers." Bakhtin pointed out that when we converse, we must keep in mind not only what has been said but what will probably be said. His notion of "intertextuality" is relevant here, because it is the term that deals with what has been said and written, and in our dialogue we often draw upon other texts, just as artists and writers and filmmakers draw on previous texts in their work.

When we come to the third means of understanding difference, the cultural one, Hall mentions the work of the British social anthropologist Mary Douglas, who bases many of her ideas on works by the French sociologist Emile Durkheim and the French anthropologist Claude Lévi-Strauss. For Douglas, difference is necessary since it is behind the classification systems we create to make sense of the world. And basic to this classificatory system is the matter of binary oppositions, which are needed if we are to be able to establish differences between things in order to classify them. We should recognize that oppositions play an

Representation and Difference

important part in the way we make sense of our everyday experiences and of mediated texts of all kinds—such as separating characters into heroes and villains, for example.

The fourth explanation of difference that Hall deals with is psychoanalytic in nature and stems from the role of others (parents, siblings, friends, lovers) in our psychic lives. The way we define ourselves, socially and sexually, Freud theorizes, is connected to our childhoods and, for Freud, to the way we deal with our Oedipal problems. Freud's theories about how young boys and girls develop (connected with his concepts of castration anxiety and penis envy) are very controversial, I should point out, even though the notion of an unconscious is generally accepted, not only by Freudians but also by Jungians and scholars in many different disciplines.

This analysis of difference focuses on the different ways people strive to find meaning in objects, relationships, mass-mediated texts, works of art, and life. We are, whatever else we may be, creatures who seek to understand ourselves and the world we live in, and to help us with this task we have created language and different kinds of arts carried by different kinds of media. Even the brave new digital world we live in, with its cell phones and cameras and gigantic television screens, is based on a binary opposition—between 1s and 0s, between "off" and "on."

Let me conclude this discussion with a Zen joke.

Question: What's the difference between a crocodile?

Answer: It swims in the water but not on the land!

Appendix: Learning Games and Activities

I should point out that a number of the selections found in this book can be used in conjunction with my book *Games and Activities for Media, Communication, and Cultural Studies Students*. These selections and the games are shown in the chart below:

Selection	Game in Games & Activities Book
Saussure	Signifier/Signified Game
Lakoff/Johnson	Metaphor Game
Lévi-Strauss	Lévi-Strauss and Paradigmatic Analysis
Cortese, Haug	Ad Agency: Pitching a Print Advertisement
Bettelheim	Functional Fairy Tales
Lesser	The Id, Ego, Superego Game
Cox	The Myth Game
Fry	The Comedy Calculator Experiment
Sapirstein, Jung	Time Capsules
Douglas	Sacred Roots

Let me offer learning games and activities derived for some of the other selections in this book.

These learning games should be played as follows (to the extent it is possible):

1. Break the class into small groups of three students (optimal).
2. Ask the students to cooperate in playing the game.
3. Appoint one student as a "scribe" to write down the conclusions of the team.
4. Have the scribe report what conclusions or answers the team reached.
5. Discuss the different answers or conclusions the various teams reached.

New Learning Games and Activities

1. Find a print advertisement with text and images and analyze it in terms of its signifiers, signifieds, metaphors, metonymies, and symbols. Choose one that is "rich"—that is full of symbols and such.

2. A person smiles. From a semiotic (facial expression) perspective, how many different meanings might that smile have? How do we know which meanings are correct? Can we know? What role does context play here?

3. Locate the scripts for a sitcom and a serious drama. Analyze the dialogue in the scripts in terms of the theories about conversation discussed in this book. You can also do this game with a comic book, analyzing the dialogue in the balloons (and the lettering, the shape of the balloons, etc.).

4. List six common activities in which people participate. Then consider the latent functions of these activities. Some activities to consider (but you can add your own to the list):

Watching a football game on television	Going out to eat in a fast-food restaurant
Listening to music on a device such as an iPod	Text-messaging a friend
Going to church, synagogue, or mosque	Playing a video game online

5. Consider the logical implications of the following metaphors (though you can add your own to this list):

I am a camera.	Life is a dream.
Happiness is a warm puppy.	I am an empty seashell.

6. Use the Berger model of art/artist/audience/America/media to deal with a film, a specific music video, or a novel. Pay attention to the role the medium plays in the creation of the text and its dissemination.

7. Look for examples of intertexuality in the following film texts:

Matrix	*Lord of the Rings*
Star Wars	*Blade Runner*

8. Find a script of a narrative (such as a film or television show), and use Tannen's ideas to see how men and women use language differently. You can also do this using dialogue in comic strips and dialogue in novels.

9. Analyze a buddy film featuring a black and a white actor team in terms of bell hooks's ideas about race and mass culture. You can also record several hours on prime-time television and count the number of men and women, people of color, and other groups to see who is overrepresented and who is underrepresented.

10. Record some commercials. Then turn off the sound and examine them in terms of the facial expressions and body language of the actors and actresses in the commercial. How does their body language connect to spoken lan-

guage or printed matter in the commercial? What techniques are used to sell the products and services being advertised?

11. If there are hidden meanings found in everyday objects, analyze some of them to find those hidden meanings (latent functions). Topics to consider:

Microwave ovens   Birkenstock sandals
Trash compactors   Low-fat lattes
Electric knives   Low-rider jeans
Electric toothbrushes   iPods

12. Write an advertisement for each of the members of your team. What should you emphasize? What is your audience? How will you reach them? Consider the language, images, and other devices you can use. Write an advertisement for the course you are taking in which you are playing these learning games.

13. Roland Barthes comes back to life in America to write a new *Mythologies*. What topics would he write about? Write about one of them from a Barthesian perspective.

14. Marshall McLuhan comes back to life. What would he say about

Cellphones   Rap music
iPods   Reality television
Text messaging   Postmodernism
Smart mobs   *Saturday Night Live*

15. You are appointed editor of POMO: *The Magazine of American Postmodernism*. Find a postmodern building or mass-mediated text (film, television show, commercial) and write an essay in which you explain the ways it is postmodern and discuss what its impact might be on American culture and society.

16. Create a new video game concept. Describe its features. What will you call it? What will happen in it? How will you reach its target audience?

17. You are appointed president of CBS Network. Think up a new genre that will draw large audiences. What are the characteristics of the new genre? What attributes in it will appeal to audiences? What will you call your first show? Who will be in it? What will happen in it? (You can deal with this matter in just a few sentences, summarizing the action.)

18. Keep a diary for one day of all the narrations to which you are exposed. To the extent you can, list the time of the narration, what medium carried it, how long it lasted, and what it was about. What conclusions do you draw from this list? Share your list with your team members. What conclusions do you draw about each list and the lists in general?

19. Find some good jokes and show how supporters of each of the four theories (superiority, masked aggression, incongruity, and communication complexities) would analyze each joke. Then use the list of forty-five techniques to find the various techniques in the jokes.

Glossary

aberrant decoding   When audiences decode, make sense of, or interpret texts in ways that differ from the ways the creators of these texts expect them to be decoded, we have aberrant decoding. Aberrant decoding is the rule, rather than the exception, when it comes to the mass media, according to the semiotician Umberto Eco.

administrative research   Administrative research deals with ways of making communication by organizations and other entities more efficient and more effective. It makes use of statistics and other empirical means of collecting data. Administrative research contrasts with critical research, which has more of an interest in social and economic justice, politics, and related considerations.

agenda setting   This theory argues that the institutions of mass communication don't determine what we think, but do determine what it is that we think about. In so doing, they set an agenda for our decision making and thus influence, in important ways, our social and political life.

artist   For our purposes an artist is not only someone who does paintings or sculptures or plays musical instruments, but anyone involved in the creation or performance of any kind of text—especially mass-mediated texts.

attitude   Social psychologists use the term to refer to a relatively enduring state of mind in a person about some phenomenon or aspect of experience. Attitudes usually are either positive or negative, have direction, and involve thoughts, feelings, and behaviors (tied to these attitudes).

audience   When we deal with audiences of the mass media, we mean people who watch a television program, listen to a radio program, attend a film or some kind of artistic performance (symphony, rock band, etc.). The members of an audience may be together in one room or in many different places. In the case of television, we often have families in which each member of the family watches different programs from his or her own set. In technical terms, audiences are addressees who receive mediated texts sent by some addresser.

broadcast   We use the term to deal with texts that are made available over wide areas through the use of radio or television signals. Broadcasting differs from other forms of distributing texts such as cable casting, which uses cables, and satellite transmission, which requires "dishes" to capture signals sent by the satellites.

class   A class, from a linguistic standpoint, is any group of things that has something in common. We use the term *class* to refer to social classes or, more literally, socioeconomic classes: groups of people who differ from other groups in terms of income and lifestyle. Marxist theorists argue that there is a ruling class that shapes the ideas of the proletariat, the working classes.

codes By *codes* we mean systems of symbols, letters, words, sounds, or whatever, that generate meaning. Language is a code. It uses combinations of letters that we call *words* to mean certain things. The relation between the word and the thing the word stands for is arbitrary, based on convention. In some cases, the term *code* is used to describe hidden meanings and disguised communications.

cognitive dissonance Dissonance refers to sounds that clash with one another, are unpleasant, and cause pain and anxiety in listeners. According to social scientists, people wish to avoid ideas that challenge the ones they hold—ideas that create conflict and other disagreeable feelings. Cognitive dissonance refers, then, to ideas that conflict with ones people hold and that generate psychological anxiety and displeasure. People seek to avoid cognitive dissonance.

collective representations The great French sociologist Emile Durkheim used this concept to deal with the fact that people are both individuals, pursuing their own aims, and social animals, who are guided by the groups and societies in which they find themselves, and whose ideas come from these groups. Collective representations are, broadly speaking, texts that reflect the beliefs and ideals of groups and other collectivities.

communication For our purposes, communication is a process that involves the transmission of messages from senders to receivers. We often make a distinction between communication using language, or verbal communication, and communication using facial expressions, body language and other means, or nonverbal communication.

communications Communications, the plural of the term *communication*, refers to messages, to what is communicated, in contrast to the process of communication, described above.

concept We understand *concept* to be a general idea or notion that explains or helps us understand some phenomenon or phenomena. For example, Freud uses the concepts "id," "ego," and "superego" in his psychoanalytic theory to explain the way the human psyche operates.

consolidation This refers to the fact that most of the media companies are now controlled by an increasingly smaller number of corporations.

consumer culture We understand the term to mean a society where the focus is upon personal consumption rather than social programs and other public goods such as education and health.

critical research Critical approaches to media are essentially ideological; they focus on the social, economic, and political dimensions of the mass media and the way they are used by organizations and others allegedly to maintain the status quo rather than to enhance equality. This contrasts with *administrative research*.

cultivation theory Cultivation theory argues that television dominates the symbolic environment of its audiences and gives people false views of what reality is like. That is, television "cultivates" or reinforces certain beliefs in its viewers, such as the notion that society is permeated by violence and we live in a dangerous world.

cultural homogenization The term *cultural homogenization* is used to suggest that the media of mass communication are destroying Third World cultures and regional cultures in specific countries, leading to a cultural sameness, standardization, or "homogenization."

cultural imperialism (also media imperialism)   Supporters of this theory, sometimes known as "Coca-colonization," argue that the flow of media products (such as films and television programs) and popular culture from the United States, and a few other capitalist countries in Western Europe, to the Third World is colonizing people in these countries. Along with these texts and popular culture, it is alleged that values and beliefs (and, most importantly, bourgeois capitalist ideology) are also being transmitted, leading to the domination of people in Third World countries.

culture   From an anthropological perspective, culture involves the transmission from generation to generation of specific ideas, arts, customary beliefs, ways of living, behavior patterns, institutions, and values. When the term *culture* is applied to the arts, it generally is used to specify "elite" kinds of artistic works, such as operas, poetry, classical music, serious novels, and so on.

defense mechanisms   In Freud's psychoanalytic theory, defense mechanisms are methods used by the ego to defend itself against pressures from the id or impulsive elements in the psyche and superego elements such as conscience and guilt. Some of the more common defense mechanisms are repression (barring unconscious instinctual wishes, memories, etc., from consciousness), regression (returning to earlier stages in one's development), ambivalence (a simultaneous feeling of love and hate for some person), and rationalization (offering excuses to justify one's actions).

demographics   Demographics refers to similarities found in selected groups of people in characteristics such as religion, gender, social class, ethnicity, occupation, place of residence, and age.

deviance   Individuals who are members of deviant groups have values and beliefs and behavior patterns that are different from (that is, they deviate from) those of most people in society.

dialogic   The term comes from the Russian theorist Bakhtin, who argued that communication should be seen as similar in nature to a dialogue, in contrast to a one-sided monologue. The focus is upon the interaction of two or more individuals in the development of language.

digital   "Digital systems," as Peter Lunenfeld explains things, "translate all input into binary structures of Os and 1s, which can then be stored, transferred, or manipulated at the level of numbers of 'digits' (so called because etymologically, the word descends from the digits on our hand with which we count out those numbers)" (Lunenfeld 1999, xv).

disfunctional (also dysfunctional)   Something is disfunctional if it contributes to the breakdown or destabilization of the entity in which it is found.

ego   In Freud's theory of the psyche, the ego functions as the executant of the id and as a mediator between the id and the superego. The ego is involved with the perception of reality and the adaptation to reality.

ethical media criticism   Ethics is that branch of philosophy that involves our sense of what is moral and correct, and ethical critics deal with the texts they analyze in terms of the moral aspects of what happens in the texts and the possible impact of these texts on others.

ethnocentrism   This refers to the notion that one's own ethnic group's ideas, customs, beliefs, and way of life are better that those of other ethnic groups.

expressive theory of art   The expressive theory of art holds that the principle function of art is to express the feelings, beliefs, and emotions of the creator of texts and works of art.

fairy tale   Fairy tales are understood to be stories for children, passed down through the millenia, with characters who are typical and common rather than unique and who embody good or evil in direct and apparent ways. As Bruno Bettelheim explained in his book *The Uses of Enchantment: The Meaning and Importance of Fairy Tales* (1976), these tales help children deal with conflicts and anxieties and existential dilemmas they face. He contrasts fairy tales with myths, which deal with great heroes and heroines who generally die or are destroyed, and which make demands on readers and listeners. In contrast, fairy tales have happy endings. (See myth.)

false consciousness   For Marxists, false consciousness refers to mistaken ideas that members of the proletariat (and other classes as well) have about their class, status, and economic possibilities. These ideas help maintain the status quo and are of great use to the ruling class, which wants to avoid changes in the social structure. Marx argued that the ideas of the ruling class are always the ruling ideas in society.

fashion   Fashion is a form of collective behavior that covers matters such as changes in styles of dress; evaluations of consumer objects such as furniture, kitchen appliances, and house design; and social customs. Why certain styles of dress or kinds of automobiles become stylish or "hot" is a subject about which there is considerable controversy.

feminist criticism   Feminist criticism, generally speaking, focuses on the roles given to women in texts and the way they are portrayed in general in texts of all kinds, but especially mass-mediated ones. Feminist critics argue that women are typically used as sexual objects and are portrayed stereotypically in texts, and that this has negative effects not only on women but also on men.

focal points   Focal points refer to the five general topics or subject areas we can concentrate upon in dealing with mass communication. These are the work of art or text, the artist, the audience, America or the society, and the media.

formula   In narrative theory, a formulaic text refers to a text with conventional characters and actions that audiences are familiar with. Genre texts, such as westerns, sitcoms, detective stories, science fiction adventures, and romances, are highly formulaic.

functional   In sociological theory, the term *functional* refers, broadly speaking, to the contribution an institution makes to the maintenance of society. Something is functional if it helps maintain the system in which it is found.

functional alternative   The term *functional alternative* refers to an entity that can be used as an alternative to something—that is, it takes the place of something else. For example, professional football games can be seen as a functional alternative to religious services on Sundays.

game   A game is conventionally understood to be an activity that people do, generally for enjoyment and entertainment, that has stated rules of procedure that all players must obey.

gatekeepers   In the news world, gatekeepers are editors and others who determine what stories are used in newspapers or news programs on the electronic media. Literally speaking, gatekeepers stand at some gate and determine who or what goes through it. Thus, these gatekeepers determine what news stories we get, but in a broader sense, gatekeepers decide what programs and films we see, what songs we hear, and so on.

gender   This term refers to the sexual category of an individual, masculine or feminine, and to behavioral traits customarily connected with each category.

genre   *Genre* is a French term that means "kind" or "class." In this book it refers to the kind of formulaic texts found in the mass media: soap operas, news shows, sports programs, horror shows, detective programs, and so on.

hypodermic needle theory of media   The hypodermic theory, generally discredited now, holds that all members of an audience "read" a text the same way and get the same things out of it. Media are seen as being like a hypodermic needle, injecting the message into one and all. Some theorists talk about interpretive communities, which suggest that groups of people can get similar messages from texts.

hypothesis   A hypothesis is a notion that is assumed to be true for the purposes of discussion or argument or further investigation. It is, in a sense, a guess or supposition that is used to explain some phenomenon.

icon   In Peirce's theory of semiotics, an icon is a sign whose meaning is evident because it resembles something. Thus, a photograph is an icon. The simplified drawings of men and women found outside toilets are commonly used icons.

id   In Freud's theory of the psyche (technically known as his structural hypothesis) the "id" is that element of the psyche that is the representative of a person's drives. Freud called it, in *New Introductory Lectures on Psychoanalysis*, "a chaos, a cauldron of seething excitement." It also is the source of energy, but lacking direction, it needs the ego to harness it and control it. In popular thought, it is connected with impulse, lust, "I want it all now" kind of behavior.

ideology   An ideology can be understood to mean a logically coherent, integrated explanation of social, economic, and political matters that helps establish the goals and direct the actions of some group or political entity. People act (and vote or don't vote) on the basis of some ideology they hold, even though they may not have articulated it or thought much about it.

image   Defining image is extremely complicated. I define an image as a combination of signs and symbols—what we find when we look at a photograph, a film still, a shot of a television screen, a print advertisement, or just about anything. The term is also used for mental as well as physical representations of things. Images often have powerful emotional effects on people and historical significance, as my discussion of 9/11 demonstrates. Two recent books that deal with images in some detail are Kiku Adato's *Picture Perfect: The Art and Artifice of Public Image Making* and Paul Messaris's *Visual Literacy: Image, Mind and Reality*.

index   In Peirce's theory of semiotics, indexical signs convey meaning by means of a cause-and-effect relationship. Smoke generally indicates fire, and thus smoke is an indexical sign.

language   Language can be understood to mean a system of rules and conventions regarding words and communication that is understood by members of a group or community. In his *Course in General Linguistics*, Saussure writes "language is a system of interdependent terms in which the value of each term results solely from the simultaneous presence of others ..." (1966, 114). It is their relative position that gives words and signs meaning. As he explains, "In language there are only differences" (126).

latent functions   Latent functions are understood to be hidden, unrecognized, and unintended functions of some activity, entity, or institution. They are contrasted by social scientists with manifest functions, which are recognized and intended.

lifestyles   This term, which means, literally, "style of life," refers loosely to the way people live—to the decisions they make about such matters as how to decorate their apartment or home (and where it is located), what kind of car they drive, what kind of clothes to wear, what kinds of foods to eat (and which restaurants they dine at), and where they go for vacations.

limited effects (of media)   Some mass communication theorists argue that the mass media have limited or relatively minor effects in the scheme of things. They cite research that shows, for example, that effects from media don't tend to be long lasting and argue that the notion that mass media have strong effects has not been demonstrated. This notion is no longer as prominent as it used to be.

manifest functions   The manifest functions of some activity, entity, or institution are those that are obvious and intended. Manifest functions contrast with latent functions, which are hidden and unintended. The manifest function of television viewing may be entertainment, while the latent function might involve becoming more materialistic.

mass   For our purposes, *mass* as in "mass communication" refers to a large number of people who are the audience for some communication. There is considerable disagreement about how to understand the term *mass*. In earlier years, theorists said a "mass" is composed of individuals who are heterogeneous, do not know one another, are alienated, and do not have a leader. Others attack these notions, saying they are not based on fact or evidence but on speculative theories that have not been verified.

mass communication   Mass communication refers to the transfer of messages, information, texts, and so on for a sender of some kind to a large number of people, a mass audience. This transfer is done through the technologies of the mass media—newspapers, magazines, television programs, films, records, computers and CD ROMs, and so on. The sender often is a person in some large media organization, the messages are public, and the audience tends to be large and varied.

media aesthetics   When applied to the media, aesthetics involves the way technical matters such as lighting, sound, music, kinds of shots and camera work, editing, and related matters in texts affect the way members of audiences react to these texts.

medium (plural: media)   A medium is understood to be a means of delivering messages, information, and texts to audiences. There are different ways of classifying the media. Some of the most common are print (newspapers, magazines, books, billboards), electronic (radio, television, computers, CD ROMS), and photographic (photographs, films, videos). But there are other ways of classifying them that are described in this book.

metacommunication   Metacommunication is communication about communication. The term *meta* suggests beyond, above, or more comprehensive.

metaphor   A metaphor is a figure of speech that conveys meaning by analogy. We must realize that metaphors are not confined to poetry and literary works but, according to some linguists, are the fundamental way in which we make sense of things and find meaning in the world. A simile is a weak form of metaphor that uses either "like" or "as" in making an analogy. Metaphors can be communicated by visual images; they aren't dependent upon language.

metonymy   According to linguists, metonymy is a figure of speech that conveys information by association and is, along with metaphor, one of the most important ways people convey information to one another. We tend not to be aware of our use of metonymy, but whenever we use association to get an idea about something (Rolls Royce = wealthy) we are thinking metonymically. A form of metonymy that involves seeing a whole in terms of a part or vice versa is called *synecdoche*. Using "The White House" to stand for the presidency is an example of synecdoche. Like metaphors, metonymies can be communicated visually, using images.

mimetic theory of art   This theory, dating from Aristotle's time, suggests that art is an *imitation* of reality. Art, then, is a "mirror" of life, which explains why we can find so much about society and people in texts. Some theorists suggest that art is not a mirror but a lamp that projects the reality of the creators behind texts.

model   In the social sciences, models are abstract representations that show how some phenomenon functions. Theories are typically expressed in language, but models tend to be represented graphically and often use statistics or mathematics. Denis McQuail and Sven Windahl define *model* in *Communication Models for the Study of Mass Communication* as "a consciously simplified description in graphic form of a piece of reality. A model seeks to show the main elements of any structure or process and the relationships between these elements" (1993, 2).

modernism   *Modernism* is the term critics use to deal with the arts (architecture, literature, visual arts, dance, music, and so on) in the period from approximately the turn of the century until around the sixties. The modernists rejected narrative structure for simultaneity and montage and explored the paradoxical nature of reality. Some of the more important modernists are T. S. Eliot, Franz Kafka, James Joyce, Pablo Picasso, Henri Matisse, and Eugene Ionesco. The period after modernism is called postmodernism.

myth   Myths are stories, generally didactic and usually tragic, found in specific groups of people or nations, about superheroic figures and gods and goddesses. Myths tend to reflect the worldview of the people who tell them and are used to explain the origin of the world, natural phenomena, and customary behaviors. The myth of Oedipus was of particular interest to Freud, who used it to explain human development.

narrative   A narrative is a story, generally sequential in nature, with a beginning, a middle (where complications arise), and a resolution. Narratives of one sort or another (such as sitcoms, mysteries, action-adventure shows, dramas, and science fiction films) dominate our media but also are found in jokes, personal conversations, and our dreams. Social scientists point out that a great deal of what people learn about life comes from narratives.

narrowcasting　A medium like radio, which has stations that tend to focus on discrete groups of people, is said to be narrowcasting. This contrasts with broadcasting media, like television, which try to reach as large an audience as possible.

nonverbal communication　A great deal of communication comes from nonverbal phenomena. Our body language, facial expressions, style of dress, style of wearing our hair, and so on are examples of our communicating feelings and attitudes (and a sense of who we are) without using words. Even in conversations, a great deal of the communication comes from our body language.

paradigmatic　I use the term here to represent a typical example of something. It also refers to the theories of Claude Lévi-Strauss, who used it to refer to a pattern of bipolar oppositions found in texts such as myths.

phallic symbol　An object that resembles the penis either by shape or function is described as a phallic symbol. Symbolism is a defense mechanism of the ego that permits hidden or repressed sexual or aggressive thoughts to be expressed in a disguised form. For a discussion of this topic see Freud's book *An Interpretation of Dreams*. Many print advertisements and television commercials make use of phallic symbols to excite people emotionally.

political cultures　According to the late political scientist Aaron Wildavsky, all democratic societies have four political cultures and need these four cultures to balance off one another. These political cultures Wildavsky identified are individualists, elitists, egalitarians, and fatalists. A political culture is made up of people who are similar in terms of their political values and beliefs, and for Wildavsky, in relation to group boundaries and rules and prescriptions they observe.

popular　The term *popular* is one of the most difficult terms used in discourse about the arts and the media. Literally speaking, *popular* means appealing to large numbers of people. It comes from the Latin term *popularis*, "of the people."

popular culture　*Popular culture* is a term that identifies certain kinds of mass-mediated texts that appeal to large numbers of people—that is, that are popular. But mass communication theorists often identify (or should we say confuse) "popular" with "mass" and suggest that if something is popular, it must, by necessity, be of poor quality, appealing to the mythical "lowest common denominator." Popular culture is generally held to be the opposite of "elite" culture—arts that require certain levels of sophistication and refinement to be appreciated, such as ballet, opera, poetry, classical music, and so on. Postmodern theorists reject this popular culture/elite culture polarity.

pornography　This term is almost impossible to define. Generally speaking, pornography is held to be material that is sexually explicit and is meant to arouse sexual excitement. The root of the term, *porne*, means "prostitute" in Greek.

postmodernism　We Americans are, some theorists suggest, living in a postmodern era—and have been doing this since the 1960s, more or less. Literally speaking, the term *postmodernism* (sometimes written as *post-modernism*) means "after modernism," the period from approximately 1900 to the 1960s. Postmodernism is characterized by, as a leading theorist of the subject, Jean-Francois Lyotard, put it, "incredulity toward metanarratives" (1984, xxiv). By this he means that the old philosophical belief systems or metanarratives that had helped people order their lives and societies no longer are accepted or given credulity. This leads to a period in which, some have suggested, anything goes.

power   Power is, politically speaking, the ability to implement one's wishes as far as policy in some entity is concerned. When we use the term to discuss texts, we use it to describe their ability to have an emotional impact upon people—readers, viewers, or listeners, and sometimes to have social, economic, and political consequences.

psychoanalytic theory   Freud's psychoanalytic theory is based on the notion that the human psyche has what he called an "unconscious," which is inaccessible to individuals, ordinarily speaking (unlike consciousness and the preconscious), and which continually shapes and affects our mental functioning and behavior. We can symbolize this by imagining an iceberg: The tip of the iceberg, showing above the water, represents consciousness. The part of the iceberg we can see, just below the surface of the water, represents the preconscious. And the rest of iceberg (most of it, which cannot be seen but we know is there) represents the unconscious. We cannot access this area of our psyches because of repression. Freud also emphasized matters such as sexuality and the role of the Oedipus complex in everyone's lives and in our social relations.

psychographics   In marketing this term is used to deal with groups of people who have similar psychological characteristics or profiles. The VALS (values and life styles) typology is an example of a marketing system based on psychographics. Psychographics differ from demographics that marketers use to focus upon social and economic characteristics that some people have in common.

public   Instead of the term *popular culture*, some theorists use the terms *the public arts* or *public communication* to avoid the negative connotations of the terms *mass* and *popular*. A public is a group of people, a community. We can contrast public acts—those meant to be known to the community—with private acts, which are not meant to be known to others. But private acts often have social and public consequences.

rationalization   In Freudian thought, a rationalization is a defense mechanism of the ego that creates an excuse to justify some action (or inaction when an action is expected). Ernest Jones, who introduced the term, used it to describe logical and rational reasons that people give to justify behavior that is really caused by unconscious and irrational determinants.

reader response theory (also reception theory)   Reader response theory suggests that readers (a term used very broadly to cover people who read books, watch television programs, go to films, and listen to texts on the radio) play an important role in the realization of texts. Texts, then, function as sites for the creation of meaning by readers, and different readers interpret a given text differently. How differently is a matter of considerable conjecture.

relativism   In philosophical thought, relativism refers to the belief that truth is relative and not absolute, that there are no universally accepted objective standards. In ethical thought, relativism suggests there are no absolutes of morality and ethics. Thus, for relativists, different cultures have different ways of living and practices that are as valid as any others. That is, morality and ethical behavior are relative to particular groups and cannot be generalized to include all human beings. This contrasts with the notion that there are ethical absolutes or universals—which can and should be applied to everyone.

representation   In his book *Representation: Cultural Representations and Signifying Practices*, media theorist Stuart Hall explains that meaning is essentially produced through language and images and communicated to others. He writes, "Representation connects meaning and language to culture. . . . Representation *is* an essential part of the process by which meaning is produced and exchanged between members of a culture" (1997, 15).

role   A role, as sociologists use the term, is a way of behavior that we learn in a given society and that is held to be appropriate to a particular situation. A person generally plays many roles with different people during a given day, such as husband (marriage), parent (family), and worker (job).

secondary modeling systems   Language, according to Yuri Lotman, is our primary modeling system. Works of art that use phenomena such as myths and legends function as secondary modeling systems; they are secondary to language, that is.

selective attention (or selective inattention)   People have a tendency to avoid messages that conflict with their beliefs and values. One way people do this is by selective attention—by avoiding or not paying attention to messages that would generate cognitive dissonance.

semiotics   The term *semiotics* means, literally, "the science of signs." *Semeion* is the Greek term for "sign." A sign is anything that can be used to stand for something else. According to C. S. Peirce, one of the founders of the science, a sign "is something which stands to somebody for something in some respect or capacity."

serial texts   We call texts that continue on for long periods of time *serial texts*. Good examples are comic strips, soap operas, and other television narratives that are on for extended periods of time. Serial texts pose problems for critics: What is the text and how do we deal with it?

sign   In semiotic theory, a sign is a combination of a *signifier* (sound, object) and a *signified* (concept). The relationship between the signifier and the signified is arbitrary, based on convention. Signs are anything that can be used to stand for something else.

socioeconomic class   Socioeconomic class is a categorization of people according to their incomes and related social status and lifestyles. In Marxist thought, there are ruling classes that shape the consciousness of the working classes, and history is, in essence, a record of class conflict.

social controls   Social controls are ideas, beliefs, values, and mores people get from their societies that shape their beliefs and behavior. People are both individuals, with certain distinctive physical and emotional characteristics and desires, and also, at the same time, members of societies, as Emile Durkheim pointed out. And people are shaped, to a certain degree, by the institutions found in these societies.

socialization   This term refers to the processes by which societies teach individuals how to behave: what rules to obey, what roles to assume, and what values to hold. Socialization was traditionally done by the family, by educators, by religious figures, and by peers. The mass media seem to have usurped this function to a considerable degree nowadays, with consequences that are not always positive. Anthropologists use the term *enculturation* for the process by which an individual is taught cultural values and practices.

spiral of silence   This theory, developed by a German scholar Elisabeth Noelle-Neumann, argues that people who hold views that they think are not widely held (whether this is correct or not) tend to keep quiet, while those who hold views that they believe are widely accepted tend to state their views strongly, leading to a spiral in which certain views tend to be suppressed while others gain increased prominence.

stereotypes   Commonly held, simplistic, and inaccurate group portraits of categories of people are called *stereotypes*. These stereotypes can be positive, negative, or mixed, but usually they are negative in nature. Stereotyping always involves making gross overgeneralizations. (All Mexicans, Chinese, Jews, African Americans, WASPs, Muslims, Americans, lawyers, doctors, professors, and so on are held to have certain characteristics, usually something negative.)

structuralism   This approach, derived from the theories of Ferdinand de Saussure and exemplified in the work of anthropologist Claude Lévi-Strauss, focuses on the relationship among elements in some system or larger entity. Structuralists are also interested in a deep structure that underlies many phenomena. This interest in a deep structure can be used to analyze everything from architecture and foods to myths and fashions.

subculture   Subcultures are cultural subgroups whose religious practices, ethnicity, sexual orientation, beliefs, values, behaviors, and lifestyles vary in certain ways from those of the dominant mainstream culture. In any complex society, it is normal to have a considerable number of subcultures.

subliminal   This theory suggests that images, shown on television or film screens for only a small fraction of a second and generally not consciously recognized by viewers, can have effects on people exposed to these images.

superego   In Freud's theory, the superego is the agency in our psyches related to conscience and morality. The superego is involved with processes such as approval and disapproval of wishes on the basis of whether they are moral or not, critical self-observation, and a sense of guilt over wrongdoing. The functions of the superego are largely unconscious and are opposed to id elements in our psyches. Mediating between the two, and trying to balance them, are our egos.

symbol   In Peirce's theory of semiotics, a symbol is a kind of sign whose meaning is conventional—it has to be learned. Symbols generally are understood to mean something that stands for something else. The term *symbol* comes from the Greek word *symbolon*, which is defined as a token or sign. Many objects have symbolic meaning and represent something that has been repressed by the conscious mind that has sexual or religious content. In "The Importance of Dreams," psychologist Carl G. Jung writes, "What we call a symbol is a term, a name, or even a picture that may be familiar in daily life, yet that possesses specific connotations in addition to its conventional and obvious meaning" (1968, 3).

text   The term *text* is used in academic discourse to refer to, broadly speaking, any work of art in any medium. The term *text* is used by critics as a convenience—so they don't have to name a given work all the time or use various synonyms. There are problems involved in deciding what the text is when we deal with serial texts, such as soap operas or comics.

theories   Theories, as the term is conventionally understood, are expressed in language and systematically and logically attempt to explain and predict phenomena being studied. They differ from concepts, which define phenomena that are being studied, and from models, which are abstract, usually graphic in nature, and explicit about what is being studied.

typology   A typology is a classification scheme or system of categories that someone uses to make sense of some phenomena. Classification schemes are important because the way we classify things affects the way we think about them.

unconscious   According to Freudian psychoanalytic theory, there are three levels of consciousness in the human psyche: what we are conscious of; a preconscious consisting of material that can be accessed; and an unconscious, which is the major part of our psyche and which we cannot access under ordinary circumstances. What is important is that according to Freud and many other psychologists, our unconscious exercises a great deal of control over our behavior, and things buried in the unconscious are often the source of our neuroses and other psychological afflictions.

uses and gratifications theory   This theory that argues that researchers should pay attention to the way members of audiences use the media (or certain texts or genres of texts) and the gratifications they get from their use of these texts and the media. Uses and gratification researchers focus, then, on how audiences use the media and not how the media affect audiences.

values   Values are understood to be abstract and general beliefs or judgments about what is right and wrong, what is good and bad, that have implications for individual behavior and for social, cultural, and political entities. There are a number of problems with values from a philosophical point of view. First, how does one determine which values are correct or good and which aren't? That is, how do we justify values? Are values objective or subjective? Second, what happens when there is a conflict between groups, each of which holds central values that conflict with those of a different group?

video games   Video games are electronic games that are immersive and interactive—that is, they allow players to participate in the action of the game. They are played, generally speaking, on specialized consoles that have extremely powerful graphic and sound capabilities, though many video games can also be played on computers.

violence (mass-mediated)   According to Gerbner and Signorelli, media violence can be defined as "the depiction of overt physical action that hurts or kills or threatens to do so" (1988, xi). In my discussion of violence, I offer a number of different kinds and aspects of violence that have to be considered in dealing with media portrayals of violence.

youth culture   Youth cultures are subcultures formed by young people around some area of interest, usually connected with leisure and entertainment such as, for example, surfing, skateboarding, rock music, or some aspect of computers: games, hacking, and so on. Typically youth cultures adopt distinctive ways of dressing and develop institutions that cater to their needs.

Selected Bibliography

Adorno, Theodor W. *Prisms*. Translated by Samuel and Sherry Weber. Cambridge, MA: MIT Press, 1967.

———. *The Culture Industry: Selected Essays on Mass Culture*. London: Routledge, 1991.

Armstrong, Nancy. *Desire and Domestic Fiction: A Political History of the Novel*. New York: Oxford University Press, 1987.

Aronowitz, Stanley. *The Politics of Identity*. New York: Routledge, 1992.

———. *Dead Artists, Live Theories and Other Cultural Problems*. New York: Routledge, 1993.

Bakhtin, Mikhail. *The Dialogic Imagination*. Edited by Michael Holmquist. Translated by Caryl Emerson and Michael Holquist. Austin: University of Texas Press, 1981.

———. *Rabelais and His World*. Translated by Helene Iswolsky. Bloomington: Indiana University Press, 1984.

Bal, Mieke. *Narratology: Introduction to the Theory of Narrative*. Toronto: University of Toronto Press, 1985.

Barker, Martin, and Ann Beezer. *Reading into Cultural Studies*. London: Routledge, 1992.

Barthes, Roland. *Writing Degree Zero & Elements of Semiology*. Translated by Annette Lavers and Colin Smith. Boston: Beacon Press, 1970.

———. *Mythologies*. Translated by Annette Lavers. New York: Hill and Wang, 1972.

———. *Empire of Signs*. Translated by Stephen Heath. New York: Hill & Wang, 1977.

———. *Image/Music/Text*. Translated by Stephen Heath. New York: Hill & Wang, 1977.

———. *The Semiotic Challenge*. Translated by Richard Howard. New York: Hill & Wang, 1988.

Bateson, Gregory. *Steps to an Ecology of Mind*. New York: Ballantine Books, 1972.

Baudrillard, Jean. *Simulations*. Translated by Paul Foss et al. New York: Semiotext(e), 1983.

———. *The System of Objects*. Translated by James Benedict. London: Verso, 1996.

Beilharz, Peter, Gillian Robinson, and John Rundell. *Between Totalitarianism and Postmodernity: A Thesis Eleven Reader*. Cambridge, MA: MIT Press, 1992.

Beniger, James. "Who Are the Most Important Theorists of Communication?" *Communication Research*, Vol. 17, October 1990.

Bennett, Tony, and Janet Woollacott. *Bond and Beyond: The Political Career of a Popular Hero*. New York: Methuen, 1987.

Berger, Arthur Asa. *The Comic-Stripped American*. New York: Walker & Co., 1973.

———. *The TV-Guided American*. New York: Walker & Co., 1975.

———. *Signs in Contemporary Culture: An Introduction to Semiotics*. New York: Annenberg-Longman, 1984.

———. *Seeing is Believing: An Introduction to Visual Communication*. Mountain View, CA: Mayfield Publishing Co., 1989.

———. *Agitpop: Political Culture and Communication Theory*. New Brunswick, NJ: Transaction, 1990.

———. *An Anatomy of Humor*. New Brunswick, NJ: Transaction, 1993.

————. *Blind Men and Elephants: Perspectives on Humor*. New Brunswick, NJ: Transaction, 1994.

————. *Cultural Criticism: A Primer of Key Concepts*. Thousand Oaks, CA: Sage Publications, 1994.

————. *Narratives in Media, Popular Culture and Everyday Life*. Thousand Oaks, CA: Sage Publications, 1997.

————. *Postmortem for a Postmodernist*. Walnut Creek, CA: AltaMira Press, 1997.

————, ed. *The Postmodern Presence: Readings on Postmodernism in American Culture and Society*. Walnut Creek, CA: AltaMira Press, 1998.

————. *Ads, Fads and Consumer Culture*. Boulder, CO: Rowman & Littlefield, 2000.

————. *Jewish Jesters*. Cresskill, NJ: Hampton Press, 2001.

————. *The Mass Comm Murders: Five Media Theorists Self-Destruct*. Lanham, MD: Rowman & Littlefield, 2002.

————. *Video Games: A Popular Culture Phenomenon*. New Brunswick, NJ: Transaction, 2002.

————. *Media & Society: A Critical Perspective*. Lanham, MD: Rowman & Littlefield, 2003.

————. *Media Analysis Techniques*. 3rd ed. Thousand Oaks, CA: Sage Publications, 2005.

Berman, Marshall. *All That Is Solid Melts into Air: The Experience of Modernity*. New York: Touchstone Books, 1982.

Best, Steven, and Douglas Kellner. *Postmodern Theory*. New York: Guilford, 1991.

Bettelheim, Bruno. *The Uses of Enchantment*. New York: Knopf, 1976.

Blau, Herbert. *To All Appearances: Ideology and Performance*. London: Routledge, 1992.

Bogart, Leo. *Polls and the Awareness of Public Opinion*. New Brunswick, NJ: Transaction, 1985.

Bolter, Jay David, and Richard Grusin. *Remediation: Understanding New Media*. Cambridge, MA: MIT Press, 2000.

Boorstin, Daniel J. *The Image: A Guide to Pseudo-Events in America*. New York: Athaneum, 1975.

Bowlby, Rachel. *Shopping with Freud: Items on Consumerism, Feminism and Psychoanalysis*. London: Routledge, 1993.

Brenkman, John. *Straight Male Modern: A Cultural Critique of Psychoanalysis*. New York: Routledge, 1993.

Brenner, Charles. *An Elementary Textbook of Psychoanalysis*. Garden City, NY: Anchor Books, 1974.

Brown, Mary Ellen, ed. *Television and Women's Culture: The Politics of the Popular*. Newbury Park, CA: Sage Publications, 1990.

————. *Soap Opera and Woman's Talk: The Pleasure of Resistance*. Thousand Oaks, CA: Sage Publications, 1994.

Buck-Morss, Susan. *The Dialectics of Seeing: Walter Benjamin and the Arcades Project*. Minneapolis: University of Minnesota Press, 1989.

Butler, Judith. *Bodies That Matter*. New York: Routledge, 1993.

————. *Gender Trouble: Feminism and the Subversion of Identity*. New York: Routledge, 1999.

Cantor, Muriel G. *The Hollywood TV Producer*. New Brunswick, NJ: Transaction, 1988.

Cantor, Muriel G., and Joel M. Cantor. *Prime-Time Television: Content and Control*. Thousand Oaks, CA: Sage Publications, 1991.

Carey, James, ed. *Media, Myths and Narratives: Television and the Press*. Newbury Park, CA: Sage Publications, 1988.

Chandler, Daniel. *Semiotics: The Basics*. London: Routledge, 2002.

Clarke, John. *New Times and Old Enemies: Essays on Cultural Studies and America*. London: Routledge, 1992.

Collins, Richard, James Curran, Nicholas Garnham, and Paddy Scannell, eds. *Media, Culture & Society: A Critical Reader*. Newbury Park, CA: Sage Publications, 1986.

Coward, Rosalind, and John Ellis. *Language and Materialism: Developments in Semiology and the Theory of the Subject*. London: Routledge & Kegan Paul, 1977.

Crane, Diane. *The Production of Culture: Media and the Urban Arts*. Newbury Park, CA: Sage Publications, 1992.

Creed, Barbara. *The Monstrous-Feminine: Film, Feminism, Psychoanalysis*. London: Routledge, 1993.

Creedon, Pamela J. *Women in Mass Communication*. 2nd ed. Thousand Oaks, CA: Sage Publications, 1993.

Crook, Stephen, Jan Pakulski, and Malcolm Waters, eds. *Postmodernization: Change in Advanced Society*. London: Sage Publications, 1992.

Cross, Gary. *Time and Money: The Making of a Consumer Culture*. London: Routledge, 1993.

Culler, Jonathan. *Structuralist Poetics: Structuralism, Linguistics and the Study of Literature*. Ithaca, NY: Cornell University Press, 1975.

———. *Ferdinand de Saussure*. New York: Penguin Books, 1977.

———. *The Pursuit of Signs*. Ithaca, NY: Cornell University Press, 1981.

———. *On Deconstruction*. Ithaca, NY: Cornell University Press, 1982.

Danesi, Marcel, and Donato Santeramo, eds. *Introducing Semiotics: An Anthology of Readings*. Toronto: Canadian Scholars Press, 1992.

———. *Messages and Meanings: An Introduction to Semiotics*. Toronto: Canadian Scholars Press, 1994.

Davis, Robert Con, and Ronald Schleifer. *Criticism & Culture*. London: Longman, 1991.

de Certeau, Michel. *The Practice of Everyday Life*. Translated by Steven Rendall. Berkeley: University of California Press, 1984.

———. *Heterologies: Discourse on the Other*. Translated by Brian Massumi. Minneapolis: University of Minnesota Press, 1986.

Denney, Reuel. *The Astonished Muse*. New Brunswick, NJ: Transaction, 1989.

Denzin, Norman K. *Images of Postmodern Society: Social Theory and Contemporary Cinema*. London: Sage Publications, 1991.

Doane, Mary Ann. *Femmes Fatales*. New York: Routledge, 1991.

Donald, James, and Stuart Hall, eds. *Politics and Ideology*. Bristol, PA: Taylor & Francis, 1985.

Douglas, Mary. *Implicit Meanings: Essays in Anthropology*. London: Routledge & Kegan Paul, 1975.

———. *Risk and Blame: Essays in Cultural Theory*. London: Routledge, 1992.

Duncan, Hugh Dalziel. *Communication and The Social Order*. New Brunswick, NJ: Transaction, 1985.

Dundes, Alan. *Cracking Jokes: Studies in Sick Humor Cycles and Stereotypes*. Berkeley, CA: Ten Speed Press, 1987.

Durham, Meenakshi Gig, and Douglas M. Kellner, eds. *Media and Cultural Studies: Key Works*. Malden, MA: Blackwell, 2001.

Durkheim, Émile. *The Elementary Forms of the Religious Life*. New York: The Free Press, 1967.

Dyer, Richard. *The Matter of Images: Essays on Representations*. London: Routledge, 1993.

Eagleton, Terry. *Marxism and Literary Criticism*. Berkeley: University of California Press, 1976.

———. *Literary Theory: An Introduction*. Minneapolis: University of Minnesota Press, 1983.

Easthope, Antony. *Literary into Cultural Studies*. London: Routledge, 1991.

Eco, Umberto. *The Role of the Reader*. Bloomington: Indiana University Press, 1984.

Ehrmann, Jacques, ed. *Structuralism*. Garden City, NY: Anchor Books, 1970.

Elam, Keir. *The Semiotics of Theatre and Drama*. London: Methuen, 1980.

Eliade, Mircea. *The Sacred and the Profane: The Nature of Religion*. New York: Harper & Row, 1961.

Ettema, James S., and D. Charles Whitney, eds. *Audiencemaking: How the Media Create the Audience*. Thousand Oaks, CA: Sage Publications, 1994.

Ewen, Stuart. *Captains of Consciousness*. New York: McGraw-Hill, 1976.

Ewen, Stuart, and Elizabeth Ewen. *Channels of Desire: Mass Images and the Shaping of American Consciousness*. New York: McGraw-Hill.

Falk, Pasi, and Colin Cambell, eds. *The Shopping Experience*. London: Sage Publications, 1997.

Featherstone, Mike. *Consumer Culture & Postmodernism*. London: Sage Publications, 1991.

Fiske, John. *Reading the Popular*. London: Routledge, 1989.

———. *Understanding Popular Culture*. London: Routledge, 1989.

Fiske, John, and John Hartley. *Reading Television*. London: Methuen, 1978.

Fjellman, Stephen M. *Vinyl Leaves: Walt Disney World and America*. Boulder, CO: Westview, 1992.

Franklin, Sarah, Celia Lury, and Jackie Stacey. *Off-Centre: Feminism and Cultural Studies*. London: Routledge, 1992.

Freud, Sigmund. *A General Introduction to Psychoanalysis*. Translated by Joan Riviere. New York: Washington Square Press, 1960.

———. *Civilization and Its Discontents*. New York: W. W. Norton, 1962.

———. *Jokes and Their Relation to the Unconscious*. Translated by James Strachey. New York: W. W. Norton, 1963.

———. *The Interpretation of Dreams*. Translated by James Strachey. New York: Avon, 1965.

Frith, Simon. *Sound Effects: Youth, Leisure and the Politics of Rock 'n' Roll*. New York: Pantheon, 1981.

Fry, William F. *Sweet Madness: A Study of Humor*. Palo Alto, CA: Pacific Books, 1968.

Gandelman, Claude. *Reading Pictures, Viewing Texts*. Bloomington: Indiana University Press, 1991.

Garber, Marjorie. *Vested Interests: Cross-Dressing and Cultural Anxiety*. New York: Harper-Perennial, 1993.

Garber, Marjorie, Jann Matlock, and Rebecca Walkowtiz, eds. *Media Spectacles*. New York: Routledge, 1993.

Garber, Marjorie, Pratibha Parmar, and John Greyson, eds. *Queer Looks: Perspectives on Lesbian and Gay Film and Video*. New York: Routledge, 1993.

Girard, Rene. *A Theater of Envy: William Shakespeare*. New York: Oxford University Press, 1991.

Gitlin, Todd. *Inside Prime Time*. New York: Pantheon, 1985.

Goldstein, Ann, Mary Jane Jacob, Anne Rorimer, and Howard Singerman. *A Forest of Signs: Art in the Crisis of Representation*. Cambridge, MA: MIT Press, 1989.

Greenblatt, Stephen J. *Learning to Curse: Essays in Early Modern Culture*. New York: Routledge, 1992.

Grossberg, Lawrence. *We Gotta Get Out of This Place: Popular Conservatism and Postmodern Culture*. New York: Routledge, 1992.

Grossberg, Lawrence, Cary Nelson, and Paula Treicher. *Cultural Studies*. New York: Routledge, 1991.

Grotjahn, Martin. *Beyond Laughter: Humor and the Subconscious*. New York: McGraw-Hill, 1966.

Guiraud, Pierre. *Semiology*. London: Routledge & Kegan Paul, 1975.

Gumbrecht, Hansl Ulrich. *Making Sense in Life and Literature*. Translated by Glen Burns. Minneapolis: University of Minnesota Press, 1992.

Habermas, Jurgen. *The Philosophical Discourse of Modernity: Twelve Lectures*. Translated by Frederick G. Lawrence. Minneapolis: University of Minnesota Press, 1987.

——. *The New Conservatism: Cultural Criticism and the Historians' Debate*. Translated by Shierry Weber Nicholsen. Minneapolis: University of Minnesota Press, 1989.

Hall, Stuart. *The Hard Road to Renewal*. London: Verso, 1988.

——. *New Times: The Changing Face of Politics in the 1990s*. London: Routledge, 1991.

——, ed. *Representation: Cultural Representations and Signifying Practices*. London: Sage Publications, 1997.

Hall, Stuart, and Tony Jefferson, eds. *Resistance Through Rituals: Youth Subcultures in Postwar Britain*. London: Routledge, 1990. (This was originally published as *Working Papers in Cultural Studies* 7/8 from the Centre for Contemporary Cultural Studies at the University of Birmingham. For an in-depth study of Stuart Hall's work, see *Journal of Communication Inquiry*, Summer, 1986, which is devoted to him.)

Hall, Stuart, and Paddy Whannel. *The Popular Arts: A Critical Guide to the Mass Media*. Boston: Beacon Press, 1967.

Hartley, John. *The Politics of Pictures: The Creation of the Public in the Age of Popular Media*. London: Routledge, 1992.

——. *Tele-ology: Studies in Television*. London: Routledge, 1992.

Haug, W. F. *Critique of Commodity Aesthetics: Appearance, Sexuality and Advertising in Capitalist Society*. Translated by Robert Bock. Minneapolis: University of Minnesota Press, 1971.

——. *Commodity Aesthetics, Ideology & Culture*. New York: International General, 1987.

Hoggart, Richard. *The Uses of Literacy*. New Brunswick, NJ: Transaction, 1992.

hooks, bell. *Yearning: Race, Gender and Cultural Politics*. Boston: South End Press, 1990.

——. *Outlaw Culture: Resisting Representations*. New York: Routledge, 1994.

Hoover, Stewart M. *Mass Media Religion: The Social Sources of the Electronic Church*. Newbury Park, CA: Sage Publications, 1988.

Hutcheon, Linda. *The Politics of Postmodernism*. London: Routledge, 1989.

Hymes, Del, ed. *Language in Culture and Society*. New York: Harper & Row, 1964.

Iser, Wolfgang. "The Reading Process: A Phenomenological Approach." In *Modern Criticism and Theory: A Reader*, ed. David Lodge, 211–28. New York: Longman, 1988.

Jacobs, Norman, ed. *Mass Media in Modern Society*. New Brunswick, NJ: Transaction, 1992.

Jakobson, Roman. *Verbal Art, Verbal Sign, Verbal Time*. Edited by Krystyna Pomorska and Stephen Rudy. Minneapolis: University of Minnesota Press, 1985.

Jally, Sut, and Justin Lewis. *Enlightened Racism: The Cosby Show, Audiences and the Myth of the American Dream*. Boulder, CO: Westview, 1992.

Jameson, Fredric. *The Political Unconscious*. Ithaca, NY: Cornell University Press, 1981.

———. *Postmodernism, or, The Cultural Logic of Late Capitalism*. Durham, NC: Duke University Press, 1991.

———. *The Geopolitical Aesthetic: Cinema and Space in the World System*. Bloomington: Indiana University Press, 1992.

———. *Signatures of the Visible*. New York: Routledge, 1992.

Jauss, Hans Robert. *Toward an Aesthetic of Reception*. Translated by Timothy Bahti. Minneapolis: University of Minnesota Press, 1982.

Jensen, Joli. *Redeeming Modernity: Contradictions in Media Criticism*. Newbury Park, CA: Sage Publications, 1990.

Jones, Steve. *Rock Formation: Music, Technology and Mass Communication*. Thousand Oaks, CA: Sage Publications, 1992.

———, ed. *Cybersociety: Computer-Mediated Communication and Community*. Thousand Oaks, CA: Sage Publications, 1994.

Jowett, Garth, and James M. Linton. *Movies as Mass Communication*. Newbury Park, CA: Sage Publications, 1989.

Jowett, Garth S., and Victoria O'Donnell. *Propaganda and Persuasion*. 2nd ed. Thousand Oaks, CA: Sage Publications, 1992.

Jung, Carl G., ed. *Man and His Symbols*. New York: Dell, 1968.

Kellner, Douglas. *The Persian Gulf TV War*. Boulder, CO: Westview, 1992.

Korzenny, Felix, and Stella Ting-Toomey, eds. *Mass Media Effects Across Cultures*. Newbury Park, CA: Sage Publications, 1992.

Lacan, Jacques. *Ecrits: A Selection*. Translated by Alan Sheridan. New York: Norton, 1966.

Laurentis, Teresa de. *Alice Doesn't: Feminism, Semiotics, Cinema*. Bloomington: Indiana University Press, 1984.

———. *Technologies of Gender: Essays on Theory, Film and Fiction*. Bloomington: Indiana University Press, 1987.

Lazere, Donald, ed. *American Media and Mass Culture: Left Perspectives*. Berkeley: University of California Press, 1987.

Lefebvre, Henri. *Everyday Life in the Modern World*. Translated by Sacha Rabinovitch. New Brunswick, NJ: Transaction Books, 1984.

Lévi-Strauss, Claude. *Structural Anthropology*. Garden City, NY: Doubleday, 1967.

Levy, Mark R., and Michael Gurevitch, eds. *Defining Media Studies: Reflections on the Future of the Field*. New York: Oxford University Press, 1994.

Lipsitz, George. *Time Passages: Collective Memory and American Popular Culture*. Minneapolis: University of Minnesota Press, 1989.

Lotman, Yuri M. *Semiotics of Cinema*. Ann Arbor: Michigan Slavic Contributions, 1976.

———. *The Structure of the Artistic Text*. Ann Arbor: Michigan Slavic Contributions, 1977.

———. *Universe of the Mind: A Semiotic Theory of Culture*. Bloomington: Indiana University Press, 1991.

Lull, James. *Popular Music and Communication*. Thousand Oaks: Sage Publications, 1991.

Lunenfeld, Peter, ed. *The Digital Dialectic: New Essays on New Media*. Cambridge, MA: MIT Press, 1999.

Lyotard, Jean-François. *The Postmodern Condition: A Report on Knowledge*. Minneapolis: University of Minnesota Press, 1984.

MacCannell, Dean, and Juliet Flower MacCannell. *The Time of the Sign: A Semiotic Interpretation of Modern Culture*. Bloomington: Indiana University Press, 1982.

MacDonald, J. Fred. *One Nation Under Television*. Chicago: Nelson-Hall, 1994.

Mandel, Ernest. *Delightful Murder: A Social History of the Crime Story*. Minneapolis: University of Minnesota Press, 1985.

Mannheim, Karl. *Ideology and Utopia*. New York: Harvest Books, 1936.

Mattelart, Armand, and Michele Mattelart. *Rethinking Media Theory*. Translated by James A. Cohen and Marina Urquidi. Minneapolis: University of Minnesota Press, 1992.

McCarthy, Thomas. *Ideals and Illusions: On Reconstruction and Deconstruction in Contemporary Critical Theory*. Cambridge, MA: MIT Press, 1991.

McCue, Greg, with Clive Bloom. *Dark Knights: The New Comics in Context*. Boulder, CO: Westview, 1993.

McLuhan, Marshall. *The Mechanical Bride: Folklore of Industrial Man*. New York: Vanguard, 1951.

———. *Understanding Media: The Extensions of Man*. New York: McGraw-Hill, 1965.

———. *Culture Is Our Business*. New York: McGraw-Hill, 1970.

McLuhan, Marshall, and Quentin Fiore. *The Medium is the Massage*. New York: Bantam Books, 1967.

McQuail, Denis. *Media Performance: Mass Communication and the Public Interest*. Thousand Oaks, CA: Sage Publications, 1992.

———. *Mass Communication Theory: An Introduction*. Thousand Oaks, CA: Sage Publications, 1994.

Mellencamp, Patricia. *Indiscretions: Avant-Garde Film, Video and Feminism*. Bloomington: Indiana University Press, 1990.

———, ed. *Logics of Television: Essays in Cultural Criticism*. Bloomington: Indiana University Press, 1990.

Messaris, Paul. *Visual Literacy: Image, Mind & Reality*. Boulder, CO: Westview Press, 1994.

———. *Visual Persuasion: The Role of Images in Advertising*. Thousand Oaks, CA: Sage Publications, 1997.

Metz, Christian. *The Imaginary Signifier: Psychoanalysis and the Cinema*. Translated by Celia Britton. Bloomington: Indiana University Press, 1982.

Mindess, Harvey. *Laughter and Liberation*. Los Angeles: Nash Publishing, 1971.

Modleski, Tania. *Loving with a Vengeance: Mass-Produced Fantasies for Women*. New York: Routledge, 1984.

———, ed. *Studies in Entertainment: Critical Approaches to Mass Culture*. Bloomington: Indiana University Press, 1986.

———. *The Women Who Knew Too Much: Hitchcock and Feminist Theory*. New York: Routledge, 1988.

Moores, Shaun. *Interpreting Audiences: The Ethnography of Media Consumption*. Thousand Oaks, CA: Sage Publications, 1994.

Morley, David. *Family Television: Cultural Power and Domestic Leisure*. London: Routledge, 1988.

———. *Television Audiences and Cultural Studies*. London: Routledge, 1993.

Mulvey, Laura. *Visual and Other Pleasures*. Bloomington: Indiana University Press, 1989.

Murray, Janet. *Hamlet on the Holodeck: The Future of Narrative in Cyberspace*. Cambridge, MA: MIT Press, 1997.

Nash, Christopher, ed. *Narrative in Culture*. London: Routledge, 1990.

Navarro, Desiderio, ed. "Postmodernism: Center and Periphery." *The South Atlantic Quarterly* 92, no. 3 (Summer 1993).

Nichols, Bill. *Ideology and the Image: Social Representation in the Cinema and Other Media.* Bloomington: Indiana University Press, 1981.

————. *Representing Reality: Issues and Concepts in Documentary.* Bloomington: Indiana University Press, 1992.

O'Shaugnessy, Michael. *Media and Society: An Introduction.* New York: Oxford University Press, 2002.

Penley, Constance. *The Future of an Illusion: Film, Feminism and Psychoanalysis.* Minneapolis: University of Minnesota Press, 1989.

Phelan, James, ed. *Reading Narrative: Form, Ethics, Ideology.* Columbus: Ohio State University Press, 1989.

Powell, Chris, and George E. C. Paton, eds. *Humour in Society: Resistance and Control.* New York: St. Martin's Press, 1988.

Prindle, David. F. *Risky Business: The Political Economy of Hollywood.* Boulder, CO: Westview, 1993.

Propp, Vladimir. *Morphology of the Folk Tale.* 2nd ed. Austin: University of Texas Press, 1973.

————. *Theory and History of Folklore.* Translated by Ariadna Y. Martin and Richard P. Martin. Minneapolis: University of Minnesota Press, 1984.

Ramet, Sabrina Petra, ed. *Rocking the State: Rock Music and Politics in Eastern Europe and the Soviet Union.* Boulder, CO: Westview, 1993.

Real, Michael R. *Supermedia: A Cultural Studies Approach.* Newbury Park, CA: Sage Publications, 1989.

Reinelt, Janelle G., and Joseph R. Roach, eds. *Critical Theory and Performance.* Ann Arbor: University of Michigan Press, 1993.

Rheingold, Howard. *Virtual Reality.* New York: Touchstone Books, 1992.

Richardson, Glenn W., Jr. *Pulp Politics: How Political Advertising Tells the Stories of American Politics.* Lanham, MD: Rowman & Littlefield, 2003.

Richardson, Laurel. "Narrative and Sociology." *Journal of Contemporary Ethnology,* 1990.

Richter, Mischa, and Harald Bakken. *The Cartoonist's Muse: A Guide to Generating and Developing Creative Ideas.* Chicago: Contemporary Books, 1992.

Ryan, John, and William M. Wentworth. *Media and Society: The Production of Culture in the Mass Media.* New York: Allyn & Bacon, 1998.

Ryan, Michael, and Douglas Kellner. *Camera Politica: The Politics and Ideology of Contemporary Hollywood Film.* Bloomington: Indiana University Press, 1988.

Sabin, Roger. *Adult Comics: An Introduction.* London: Routledge, 1993.

Saussure, Ferdinand de. *Course in General Linguistics.* Translated by Wade Baskin. New York: McGraw-Hill, 1966.

Schechner, Richard. *The Future of Ritual: Writings on Culture and Performance.* London: Routledge, 1993.

Schickel, Richard. *The Disney Version.* New York: Avon Books, 1968.

Schneider, Cynthia, and Brian Wallis, eds. *Global Television.* Cambridge, MA: MIT Press, 1989.

Scholes, Robert. *Structuralism in Literature: An Introduction.* New Haven, CN: Yale University Press, 1974.

Schostak, John. *Dirty Marks: The Education of Self, Media and Popular Culture.* Boulder, CO: Westview, 1993.

Schwartz, Tony. *Media: The Second God.* Garden City, NY: Anchor Books, 1983.

Schwichtenberg, Cathy, ed. *The Madonna Collection*. Boulder, CO: Westview.

Sebeok, Thomas, ed. *Sight, Sound and Sense*. Bloomington: Indiana University Press, 1978.

Seldes, Gilbert. *The Public Arts*. New Brunswick, NJ: Transaction, 1994.

Shukman, Ann. *Literature and Semiotics: A Study of the Writings of Yuri M. Lotman*. Amsterdam: North-Holland Publishing, 1977.

Silverman, Kaja. *The Subject of Semiotics*. New York: Oxford University Press, 1983.

Skovman, Michael, ed. *Media Fictions*. Aarhus, Denmark: Aarhus University Press, n.d.

Steidman, Steven. *Romantic Longings: Love in America, 1830–1980*. New York: Routledge, 1993.

Stephenson, William. *The Play Theory of Mass Communication*. New Brunswick, NJ: Transaction, 1988.

Szondi, Peter. *On Textual Understanding*. Translated by Harvey Mendelsohn. Minneapolis: University of Minnesota Press, 1986.

Theall, Donald F. *The Virtual Marshall McLuhan*. Montreal and Kingston: Queen's University Press, 2001.

Todorov, Tzvetan. *The Fantastic: A Structural Approach to a Literary Genre*. Translated by Richard Howard. Ithaca, NY: Cornell University Press, 1975.

———. *Introduction to Poetics*. Translated by Richard Howard. Minneapolis: University of Minnesota Press, 1981.

Traube, Elizabeth G. *Dreaming Identities: Class, Gender, and Generation in the 1980s Hollywood Movies*. Boulder, CO: Westview, 1882.

Turner, Bryan S., ed. *Theories of Modernity and Postmodernity*. London: Sage Publications, 1990.

Van Zoonen, Liesbet. *Feminist Media Studies*. Thousand Oaks, CA: Sage Publications, 1994.

Volosinov, V. N. *Freudianism: A Critical Sketch*. Translated by I. R. Titunik. Bloomington: Indiana University Press, 1987.

Weibel, Kathryn. *Mirror Mirror: Images of Women Reflected in Popular Culture*. Garden City, NY: Anchor Books, 1977.

Wernick, Andrew. *Promotional Culture*. London: Sage Publications, 1991.

Willemen, Paul. *Looks and Frictions: Essays in Cultural Studies and Film Theory*. Bloomington: Indiana University Press, 1993.

Williams, Raymond. *Culture and Society: 1780–1950*. New York, NY: Columbia University Press, 1958.

———. *Keywords*. New York, NY: Oxford University Press, 1976.

———. *Marxism and Literature*. New York: Oxford University Press, 1977.

Williams, Rosalind. *Notes on the Underground: An Essay on Technology, Society and the Imagination*. Cambridge, MA: MIT Press, 1990.

Williamson, Judith. *Decoding Advertisements: Ideology and Meaning in Advertising*. London: Marion Boyars, 1978.

Willis, Paul. *Common Culture: Symbolic Work at Play in the Everyday Cultures of the Young*. Boulder, CO: Westview, 1990.

Wilson, Clint C., and Felix Gutierrez. *Minorities and Media: Diversity and the End of Mass Communication*. Thousand Oaks, CA: Sage Publications, 1985.

Winick, Charles. *The New People: Desexualization in American Life*. New York: Pegasus, 1968.

Wollen, Peter. *Signs and Meaning in the Cinema*. Bloomington: Indiana University Press, 1972.

————. *Raiding the Icebox: Reflections on Twentieth-Century Culture.* Bloomington: Indiana University Press, 1993.

Wright, Will. *Sixguns and Society: A Structural Study of the Western.* Berkeley: University of California Press, 1975.

Zettl, Herbert. *Sight, Sound, Motion.* Belmont, CA: Wadsworth, 1973.

Zizek, Slavoi. *Looking Awry: An Introduction to Jacques Lacan through Popular Culture.* Cambridge, MA: MIT Press, 1991.

Biographies of Key Text Authors

Espen J. Aarseth teaches in the Department of Humanistic Informatics at the University of Bergen, Norway. He has written on new technology and video games.

Roger Abrahams taught folklore and ethnography at the University of Pennsylvania. Among his books are *African Folktales*, *African American Folktales*, and *Singing the Master*.

Meyer Howard Abrams is a literary critic and scholar who taught literature at Cornell University. Among his books are *Literature and Belief* and *English Romantic Poetry*.

Aristotle (384 BC to 322 BC) is considered one of the most influential philosophers of all time. He wrote works on ethics, rhetoric, politics, and many other topics.

Mikhail Bakhtin (1895–1975) was a Russian scholar whose books on language and culture have been increasingly influential. He is the author of *Rabelais and His World* and *The Dialogic Imagination*.

Roland Barthes (1915–1980) was probably the most important cultural analyst and theoretician of recent years, known for his semiotic analyses of French culture. Among his books are *Elements of Semiology*, *Empire of Signs*, and *The Pleasure of the Text*.

Basil Bernstein (1924–2000) was professor of sociology and education at London University and an important sociolinguist. Among his books are *Pedagogy, Symbolic Control and Identity* and *Class, Codes and Control*.

Bruno Bettelheim (1903–1990) was a child psychologist who taught at the University of Chicago. Among his books are *Love Is Not Enough*, *The Empty Fortress*, and *Freud and Man's Soul*.

Lewis Carroll (1832–1898) was a pseudonym for Charles Lutwidge Dodgson, a mathematician. He wrote *Through the Looking Glass* and *The Hunting of the Snark*.

Anthony Cortese is a professor of sociology at Southern Methodist University. His research focuses on social problems and media and gender. Among his books are *Walls and Bridges: Social Justice and Public Policy* and *Ethnic Ethics: The Restructuring of Moral Theory*.

Harvey Cox teaches at Harvard University and has done research about the relationships between religion, culture, and politics. Among his many books are *The Secular City*, *The Feast of Fools*, and *The Seduction of the Spirit*.

Jonathan Culler is a professor of English and comparative literature at Cornell University. Among his books are *Structuralist Poetics* and *The Pursuit of Signs: Semiotics, Literature and Deconstruction*.

Guy Debord (1931–1994) was one of the founders of the French situationist movement. Among his books are *Comments on the Society of the Spectacle* and *Panegyric*.

Michel de Certeau (1925–1986) was a French Jesuit who wrote influential books on popular culture and media. Among his works are *Culture in the Plural*, *Heterologies*, and *The Writing of History*.

Mary Douglas is a prominent and very influential English social anthropologist who has written books such as *Natural Symbols* and *Purity and Danger*.

Paul Ekman is a psychologist who taught in the Department of Psychiatry at the University of California San Francisco Medical School. He has published many books on facial expression and emotion, such as *Emotions Revealed* and *Unmasking the Face*.

Hans Magnus Enzenberger is a German poet, novelist, and culture critic. Among his nonfiction works are *Critical Essays*, *Kiosk*, and *Raids and Reconstruction: Critical Essays on Politics, Crime and Culture*.

Martin Esslin (1918–2002) worked at the BBC for many years and after that taught at Stanford University. He was an important theater critic who wrote about the theater of the absurd and other aspects of theater. Among his books are *The Theater of the Absurd* and *An Anatomy of Drama*.

Peter Farb (1929–1980) was an anthropologist and a prolific author who wrote about many topics. Among his books are *Humankind* and *Man's Rise to Civilization*.

Sigmund Freud (1856–1939) was the founder of the psychoanalytic school of psychology and probably the most influential psychologist of all time. Among his many book are *The Interpretation of Dreams*, *Civilization and Its Discontents*, and *The Psychopathology of Everyday Life*.

Simon Frith is a sociologist at Stirling University in Scotland who specializes in rock music and its relation to youth culture. Among his books is *Sociology of Rock*.

William Fry, a psychiatrist, was associated with the Stanford University Medical School for many years. He is the coauthor (along with Melanie Allen) of *Make 'Em Laugh: Life Studies of Comedy Writers*.

Alan Gowans was a professor of the history of art at the University of Victoria in Canada. Among his books are *The Restless Art: A History of Painters and Painting, 1760–1960* and *The Comfortable House*.

Martin Grotjahn (1904–1988) was a Freudian psychiatrist who had many movie stars as patients. Among his books are *Beyond Laughter* and *My Favorite Patient*.

Stuart Hall is a prominent English cultural theorist and media critic who taught at the University of Birmingham and later at the Open University. Among his books are *Resistance Through Ritual* and *Questions of Cultural Identity*.

Wolfgang Haug is a professor of philosophy at the Free University in Berlin, Germany. He writes on media, culture and politics. Among his books is *Commodity Aesthetics, Ideology & Culture*.

bell hooks (pseudonym for **Gloria Watkins**) is a prominent black author who has dealt with issues of feminism, race, and the media in a number of books, such as *Outlaw Culture: Resisting Representation* and *Ain't I a Woman: Black Women and Feminism*.

Johan Huizinga (1872–1945) was a Dutch historian who was interested in symbolism and in cultural history. Among his books are *Erasmus* and *Homo Ludens*.

Roman Jakobson (1896–1982), a world-famous linguistics scholar, left Europe when the Nazis occupied Czechoslovakia and then taught at a number of American Universities, such as Harvard and MIT. Among his works is *Child Language, Aphasia and Phonological Universals*.

Fredric Jameson, a professor at Duke University, is a prominent theorist of postmodernism. Among his books are *Marxism and Form* and *The Geopolitical Aesthetic*.

Mark Johnson is a professor of philosophy at the University of Oregon. Among his books are *Philosophical Perspectives on Metaphor* and *The Body in the Mind: The Bodily Basis of Meaning, Imagination and Reason.*

Carl Gustav Jung (1875–1961) was one of the founders of psychoanalytic thought. He broke away from Freud in 1913 and pursued his own theories about the collective unconscious, archetypes, and personality types. Among his books are *Modern Man in Search of a Soul; Memories, Dreams and Reflections;* and *Civilization in Transition.*

George Lakoff is a professor of linguistics at the University of California, Berkeley. He is the author of *Women, Fire, and Dangerous Things: What Categories Reveal About the Mind* and numerous other books. In recent years he has become interested in language and politics.

Harold Lasswell (1902–1978) was a prominent political scientist who taught at Yale University. His ideas about communication were very influential, and his famous "formula" is still discussed and debated by scholars.

Gustave Le Bon (1841–1931) was an influential French social psychologist who wrote *The Psychology of Peoples.* His theories have implications for those studying audiences and crowd psychology.

Simon Lesser is a writer who has taught English at New York University and has held positions in the government and in industry. Among his books is *Whispered Meanings.*

Claude Lévi-Strauss (1908–1996) was probably the most influential anthropologist of recent years, who made important studies of kinship and mythology and was connected with structuralist thought. Among his books are *Structuralist Anthropology, The Savage Mind,* and *Tristes Tropiques.*

Yuri Lotman (1922–1993) was a Russian semiotician and theorist of media and culture. He was the founder of the Tartu-Moscow school of semiotics, which influenced many Russian culture analysts. Among his books are *Semiotics of Cinema* and *Universe of the Mind.*

Marshall McLuhan (1911–1980) was an important theorist of media and culture, famous for offering enigmatic concepts such as "the medium is the message" and "the global village." Among his books are *The Mechanical Bride* and *The Gutenberg Galaxy.*

Albert Mehrabian taught psychology at the University of California for many years. His area of interest includes nonverbal communication—that is, body language. Among his books are *Nonverbal Communication* and *Tactics of Social Influence.*

Neil Postman (1931–2003) taught at New York University and was a founder of the media ecology movement. Among his books are *Technopoly* and *The End of Education.*

Howard Rheingold is a futurist who has written a number of books on new technologies such as *The Virtual Community* and *Tools for Thought: The History and Future of Mind-Expanding Technology.*

Catherine Kohler Riessman taught sociology at Boston University before her retirement. Her research focuses on the relationship between narratives and personal identity. She is the author of *Divorce Talk: Women and Men Make Sense of Personal Relationships.*

Ruth P. Rubinstein is a professor of sociology at the Fashion Institute of Technology, State University of New York. Her research deals with fashion and identity. Among her books is *Society's Child: Identity, Clothing and Style*.

Milton Sapirstein is a psychiatrist who is interested in everyday life and the hidden or unconscious significance of objects and of various aspects of culture and society. Among his books is *Emotional Security*.

Ferdinand de Saussure (1857–1913), a Swiss linguistics professor, was one of the founders of the science of semiotics. His ideas influenced the development of structuralist theory and its analysis of language.

Terrence J. Sejnowski teaches biology at the University of California, San Diego. He is the coauthor (with Steven R. Quartz) of *Liars, Lovers and Heroes: What the New Brain Science Reveals About How We Become Who We Are*.

Jack Solomon is a professor of English and semiotics at the University of California, Los Angeles. Among his books are *Signs of Life in the USA: Readings on Popular Culture for Writers* and *Discourse and Reference in the Nuclear Age*.

Susan Sontag (1933–2004) was an influential, and controversial, essayist and novelist. Among her books are *Styles of Radical Will*, *Regarding the Pain of Others*, and the novel *The Benefactor*.

Robert Stein founded The Voyageur Company and led the development of more than 300 titles of films on videodisks and close to 80 DC-ROM titles. He is interested in ethics and technology.

Deborah Tannen is a professor of sociologuistics at Georgetown University who has studied gender differences in the use of language. Among her books are *Talking from 9 to 5: Women and Men at Work* and *The Argument Culture*.

Ian Watt (1917–1999) was a professor of literature at Stanford and an important literary theorist. Among his books is *The Rise of the Novel: Studies in Defoe, Richardson and Fielding*.

Index

Aarseth, Espen J., 94–96
Abrahams, Roger, 45–46
Abrams, M. H., 34–36
Abrams model: Berger model based on, 35; elements in, 34–36
advertising: bodies as commodities, 71–72; and capitalism, 71–72; creates anxiety in women, 69–70; images of women in, 68–70; models as "provocateurs," 68–70; packaging women, 68–70; role in work and sexuality, 71–72
African American speech, xiii; intertextual aspects of, 46; rap music and, 46; regressive aspects of, 45–46; role of rhyming in, 44–45; "sounding" in, 44–45; verbal combat, 44–45
Against Interpretation, 136
Age of Television, The, 114
Alice in Wonderland and Other Favorites, 8–9, 90; Humpty Dumpty on words, 8–10
American culture: advertising's impact on, 67; desexualization in, 43–44 (*see also* Miss America)
Amusing Ourselves to Death, 97, 109
Anatomy of Humor, An, 128
Aristotle, xiv, 39, 89, 127–30, 134
art: beautification, 133–35; contrasted with popular culture, 122; conviction and persuasion, 133–35; depth of art texts, 120–23; Freudian interpretations of, 136–37; functions of art and theories of art chart, 115; Gowans on four functions of, 133–35; illustration, 133–35; importance in a text, 120–22; interpretation, 136–37; long-lasting nature of, 122; Marxist interpretation, 136–37; as a means of communication, 120–23; problems

of interpretation, 136–37; relation of criticism and creativity, 137; substitute imagery, 133–35; what art is versus what art does, 133–35
Art of Comedy Writing, The, 128
Arts in Society, 76

Bakhtin, Mikhail, 37–38, 41, 46, 141–42
Bangs, Lester, 117–18
Barthes, Roland, xiv, 73–75
Bateson, Gregory, xiv
Baudrillard, Jean, 104
Beatles, The, 86
Beniger, James, xiv
Berger, Arthur Asa, 35–36, 146
Bernstein, Basil, 4, 17–18
Bettelheim, Bruno, 79–81, 112, 145
Black Looks: Race and Representation, 47–48
Blondie, 85, 117
Boas, Franz, 24
Brave New World, 97
Brenner, Charles, 63
Bruner, Jerome, 41

Cage, John, 86
Carroll, Lewis, 8, 90
Character and Culture, 11
Chekov, Anton, 120
Chomsky, Noam, xiv
Christianity and Crisis, 65
Chronicle of Higher Education, 42
Civilization and Its Discontents, 125
codes: Basil Bernstein on, 4; code model of communication, 6–7; codes as matrix to interpret world, 17–29; elaborated and restricted, 17–19, *18*; Jakobson model and, 28–30

comedy: Aristotle on, 129–32; contrasted with tragedy, 129–31, *131*; mimetic theory and, 129–30. *See also* humor

communication: avoiding cognitive dissonance, 50; dialogism and, 37–38; gender and, 42–44; Jakobson model of, 28–30; Lasswell formula, 31–33; McLuhan's theories, 36, 82–85; relation to media and culture, iii, xiii; seeking reinforcement, 50; sociology and, 20

consciousness, 12

conversation: based on rules, 40; dialogic aspects of, 41; male versus female, 42–44

conversation elements (abstract, coda, complicating action, evaluating, orientation, resolution), 39–40

Cortese, Anthony J., 67–69, 145

Course in General Linguistics, 142

Cox, Harvey, 65–67, 145

Critique of Commodity Aesthetics: Appearance, Sexuality and Advertising in Capitalist Society, 71

Crowd: A Study of the Popular Mind, 103

crowds: as audiences, 105; "hypodermic needle theory" and, 104; Le Bon's view of, 103–5; reception theory and, 104–5; theatrical representations and, 103–5

Culler, Jonathan, 14–16

culture: language and, 1; Lévi-Strauss's ideas about, 23–24; Tyler definition of, 23; unconscious and, 23–24

Cybertext: Perspectives on Ergodic Literature, 94

Debord, Guy, 138–40

de Certeau, Michel, 111–12, 116

Deep Down in the Jungle: Negro Narrative Folklore from the Streets of Philadelphia, 45

Defoe, Daniel, 76

Democracy in America, 16

Dialogic Imagination: Four Essays by M. M. Bakhtin, The, 37

dialogism: Bakhtin's theory of, 37–38; conversation and, 37–38; intertextuality and, 37–38; parody and, 38; two-way aspects of communication, 38

difference: basic to finding meaning in things, 141–43; binary oppositions and, 142; and cultural studies, 141–43; dialogical analysis and, 141–42; psychoanalytic approaches to, 141–42; Saussurean linguistics and, 141–42; social anthropological analysis, 141–42

Digital Dialectic: New Essays on New Media, 97

Don Juan, 76

Don Quixote, 76; single-minded pursuit of achievement and enterprise, *77*; and three basic themes of modern civilization, 76–78

Dostoevsky, Feodor, 123

Douglas, Mary, 20–22, 141–42, 145

dreams: archetypes and, 61; collective unconscious and, 61; displacement and condensation in, 12–13; Freud on, 12–13; Jung on symbols in, 60–62; lack of negations in, 11

Dress Codes: Meanings and Messages in American Culture, 54

Durkheim, Emile, 16, 92, 142

Eco, Umberto, 94–95

ego (mediator), 12

Ehrmann, Jacques, 21

Ekman, Paul, 52–53

Elementary Textbook of Psychoanalysis, An, 63

Eliade, Mircea, 65–66

Ellis, Havelock, 43

Emerson, Caryl, 37

Empire of Signs, 74

Enzenberger, Hans Magnus, 91–93

Essence of Christianity, The, 138

Esslin, Martin, 114–16, 122, 131

facial expressions: affective states and, 52–53; as applied semiotics, 53; cognitive activity and, 52–53; psychopathology and, 52–53; truthfulness and, 52–53. See also nonverbal communication

fairy tales: contrasted with myths, 80–81; functions for children, 79–81; psychoanalytic perspective on, 79–81; and unconscious, 79–81

Farb, Peter, 1–2

fashion: as communication, 54–56; consumer culture and, 56; gender scripts and, 55; hierarchy principle and, 55; irony of, 56; seductive principle and, 55–56; sex appropriate behavior and, 54–55

Faust, 76

Ferdinand de Saussure, 14

Feurbach, Ludwig, 138–39

Fiction and the Unconscious, 123

Flugel, J. C., 54–55

Freud, Sigmund, xiv, 11–13, 58, 64, 81, 125, 127, 136–37, 143

Frith, Simon, 117–19

Fry, William F., 126–27, 145

Garfinkel, Harold, 41

Giglioli, Pier Paolo, 17

Girard, René, 130, 131–32

Glamour, 55

Glass, Phil, 86

Gone Primitive: Savage Intellects, Modern Lives, 47

Gowans, Alan, 133–35

Great Critics: An Anthology of Literary Criticism, 129

Grotjahn, Martin, 106–8, 110, 115

Hall, Stuart, 141–43

Haug, Wolfgang, 70–72, 145

Hawthorne, Nathaniel, 123

Henry IV Part I, 3–4

Hobbes, Thomas, 127

Holquist, Michael, 37

hooks, bell, 47–48

Huizinga, Johan, 57–58

humor: incongruity theories, 127; jokes and, 126–27; as a kind of communication, 126–28; masked aggression and, 127; metacommunication and, 126–27; play frames and, 126–27; punch lines and, 126–27; relations to play, 126–27; superiority theories of, 127; techniques of humor chart, 128. See also comedy

Huxley, Aldous, 97–99, 109

Hymes, Dell, 4

id (drives), 12

Ideology and Utopia, 15, 92

Implicit Meanings: Essays in Anthropology, 20

Interpretation of Dreams, The, 12

Iser, Wolfgang, 104–5

Jakobson, Roman, xiv, 27–30, 32, 94, 95

Jakobson model (addressee, addresser, code, contact, context, emotive and referential functions, message), 28–30

James, William, 57–58

Jameson, Fredric, 86–88, 122

Johnson, Mark, 25, 145

Jung, Carl G., 58, 60–61, 143, 145

Kant, Immanuel, xiv

Labov, William, 39–40

Lakoff, George, 25, 145

language: African American speech and, xiii; categories of thought and, 4; code model of communication, 6–7; definition of, 1; development of culture and society, 2; and experience, 4; as game, 1; gender difference and, xii; human behavior and, 1; metaphor and, xii; phonemes and, 1; Sapir on, 4; and speech, 6–7; system of grammar, 1. See also African American speech; codes

Language and Social Context, 17

Language in Culture and Society, 4

Lasswell, Harold, 31–32

Lasswell formula: assumptions of, 32–33; compared to Abrams and Berger models, 36; Jakobson model and, 32; questions asked in, 31–33

Laver, James, 54–55

Le Bon, Gustave, 84, 103–5

Leninism, 86

Lesser, Simon, 123–24, 145

Lévi-Strauss, Claude, xiv, 20–24, 142, 145

Li'l Abner, 85

literature: critical approaches to, 124–25; hidden meanings in, 123–25; mimetic desire in, 132; psychic gratifications of arts, 124–25; psychoanalytic analysis of, 123–25

Lodge, David, 28, 105

Lotman, Yuri, 120–22

Lunenfeld, Peter, 97

Lyotard, Jean-François, 41, 87

Madonna, 67

Mannheim, Karl, 15, 16, 92

Marx, Karl, 124, 136–37, 139–40

Marxism: analysis of spectacles, 139–40; false consciousness, 139; ideas of ruling class are ideas of masses, 140; literary criticism, 124; mode of production and culture, 138–40; mode of production and superstructure, 140; postmodernism as late capitalism, 86–88; view of role of media in society, 139–40

McLuhan, Marshall, 35, 75, 82–85, 147

Mechanical Bride, The, 75, 84–85

media: dominated by narratives, 111–13; effects on our minds, xiii; ethical problems of digital media, 97–99; as generator of spectacles, 138–40; hot and cool, xiii, 82–84; illusion of mind's sovereignty, 91–93; importance of narratives in, xiii; industrialization of mind, 91–93; McLuhan as satirist and parodist, 84–85; mind and, 91–93; multiplayer online games, 98; portrayal of people of color, xiii; postmodernism and, xiii; power of digital, 97–99; power of rock music,

xiii; problem of decoding, 29; relation to communication, xiii; social and political effects of hot and cool media, 83–84; spectacle justifies status quo, 138–40; spectacles versus direct experience of life, 138–40; teledildonics, 98–99

Media and Cultural Studies, 138

Media Book, The, 114

Mehrabian, Albert, 49–50

Melville, Herman, 123

Merton, Robert K., 104

Messaris, Paul, 50

metaphor: based on analogy, 26–27; implications of and actions, 27; in language, thought, and action, 25–27; metonymy and, 26–27; simile and, 26

metonymy: metaphor and, 26–27; synecdoche and, 26–27

Mirror and the Lamp: Romantic Theory and the Critical Tradition, The, 34

Miss America, 65–67

Modern Criticism and Theory: A Reader, 28, 105

myth: collective representations as sign systems, 73–75; conservative ideologically speaking, 74–75; and daily French life, 73–75; hidden ideology in popular culture texts, 74–75; ideology and, 73–75; Lévi-Strauss on, 20–22; Robinson Crusoe as powerful myth, 76–78; role of public in creating, 77–78

Mythologies, 73–75, 118

narratives: Aristotle on, 39; conversation as, 39–41; dominate media, 111–13; genres of, 112–13; imprinting by, 111–13; as models for living, 111–13; as mode of reasoning, 41; as mode of representation, 41; primary way to organize experiences, 41

National Science Foundation, 53

New People: Desexualization in American Life, 43

nonverbal communication: definition of, 49–50; facial expressions and,

About the Author

Arthur Asa Berger is professor emeritus of Broadcast and Electronic Communication Arts at San Francisco State University, where he taught between 1965 and 2003. He graduated in 1954 from the University of Massachusetts, where he majored in literature and philosophy. He received an MA degree in journalism and creative writing from the University of Iowa in 1956. He was drafted shortly after graduating from Iowa and served in the U.S. Army in the Military District of Washington in Washington DC, where he was a feature writer and speech writer in the District's Public Information Office. He also wrote high school sports for the *Washington Post* on weekend evenings.

Berger spent a year touring Europe after he got out of the army and then went to the University of Minnesota, where he received a PhD in American studies in 1965. He wrote his dissertation on the comic strip *Li'l Abner*, which became his first book. In 1963–1964, he had a Fulbright to Italy and taught at the University of Milan. He spent a year as visiting professor at the Annenberg School for Communication at the University of Southern California, Los Angeles in 1984.

He is the author of numerous articles, book reviews, and more than sixty books on the mass media, popular culture, humor, and everyday life. Among his books are *The Portable Postmodernist; Shop 'Til You Drop; Media & Society; Ads, Fads and Consumer Culture; Deconstructing Travel;* and *Video Games: A Popular Culture Phenomenon*. He has also written a number of darkly humorous academic mysteries such as *The Hamlet Case, Postmortem for a Postmodernist, The Mass Comm Murders: Five Media Theorists Self-Destruct, Durkheim Is Dead: Sherlock Holmes Is Introduced to Sociological Theory* and *Mistake in Identity: A Cultural Studies Murder Mystery*. His books have been translated into seven languages and he has lectured in more than a dozen countries in the course of his career.

Berger is married, has two children and three grandchildren, and lives in Mill Valley, California. He enjoys foreign travel, lecturing on cruise ships, and dining in ethnic restaurants. He can be reached by e-mail at arthurasaberger@gmail.com or arthurasaberger @yahoo.com.

DECODER MAN